STARVING THE ANXIETY GREMLIN

by the same author

Starving the Anger Gremlin
A Cognitive Behavioural Therapy Workbook on Anger Management for Young People
Kate Collins-Donnelly
ISBN 978 1 84905 286 3
eISBN 978 0 85700 621 9

Starving the Stress Gremlin
A Cognitive Behavioural Therapy Workbook on Stress Management for Young People
Kate Collins-Donnelly
ISBN 978 1 84905 340 2
eISBN 978 0 85700 672 1

of related interest

The Panicosaurus
Managing Anxiety in Children Including Those with Asperger Syndrome
K.I. Al-Ghani
Illustrated by Haitham Al-Ghani
ISBN 978 1 84905 356 3
eISBN 978 0 85700 706 3

Helping Children to Cope with Change, Stress and Anxiety
A Photocopiable Activities Book
Deborah M. Plummer
Illustrated by Alice Harper
ISBN 978 1 84310 960 0
eISBN 978 0 85700 366 9

Focusing and Calming Games for Children
Mindfulness Strategies and Activities to Help Children to Relax, Concentrate and Take Control
Deborah M. Plummer
Illustrated by Jane Serrurier
ISBN 978 1 84905 143 9
eISBN 978 0 85700 344 7

What Children Need to be Happy, Confident and Successful
Step by Step Positive Psychology to Help Children Flourish
Jeni Hooper
ISBN 978 1 84905 239 9
eISBN 978 0 85700 483 3

Frog's Breathtaking Speech
How Children (and Frogs) Can Use the Breath to Deal with Anxiety, Anger and Tension
Michael Chissick
Illustrated by Sarah Peacock
ISBN 978 1 84819 091 7
eISBN 978 0 85701 074 2

STARVING THE ANXIETY GREMLIN

A COGNITIVE BEHAVIOURAL THERAPY WORKBOOK ON ANXIETY MANAGEMENT FOR YOUNG PEOPLE

Kate Collins-Donnelly

Jessica Kingsley *Publishers*
London and Philadelphia

First published in 2013
by Jessica Kingsley Publishers
116 Pentonville Road
London N1 9JB, UK
and
400 Market Street, Suite 400
Philadelphia, PA 19106, USA

www.jkp.com

Library of Congress Cataloging in Publication Data
Collins-Donnelly, Kate.
Starving the anxiety gremlin : a cognitive behavioural therapy workbook on anxiety management for young people / Kate Collins-Donnelly.
p. cm.
Includes bibliographical references.
ISBN 978-1-84905-341-9 (alk. paper)
1. Anxiety in adolescence--Juvenile literature. 2. Anxiety--
Juvenile literature. 3. Cognitive therapy for
teenagers--Juvenile literature. I. Title.
BF724.3.A57C65 2013
155.5'1246--dc23
2012035544

British Library Cataloguing in Publication Data
A CIP catalogue record for this book is available from the British Library

ISBN 978 1 84905 341 9
eISBN 978 0 85700 673 8

Printed and bound in Great Britain by Bell and Bain Ltd, Glasgow

The authorised representative in the EEA is Hachette Ireland,
8 Castlecourt Centre, Dublin 15, D15 XTP3, Ireland (email: info@hbgi.ie)

Contents

Acknowledgements

Firstly, I would like to thank all the young people who have bravely shared their stories and artwork in this workbook in order to help other young people realise that they are not on their own and that it is possible to get your anxiety under control. Thank you also to the young people, parents, practitioners and colleagues who have regularly reminded me of why this workbook is needed and who have motivated me to achieve what I wished to achieve through this workbook. Thank you also to Maria for her invaluable advice, knowledge, guidance and unwavering support.

About the Author

Hi! I'm Kate, and I have worked for several years providing support for children, young people and their parents as well as providing training and guidance for professionals on the emotional issues that children and young people face today. Through this work, it became evident that there was a need for a book aimed directly at children and young people on how to manage anxiety and *Starving the Anxiety Gremlin* was born.

This workbook is about empowering young people like you to starve their Anxiety Gremlin by learning more about anxiety, including how common anxiety is in young people, the types of anxiety that can be experienced, the differing ways in which anxiety can present itself, the effects it can have and why it occurs. Acquiring this knowledge is crucial to managing your anxiety as is learning about a wide range of anxiety management strategies and how to apply the ones that are relevant to you. This workbook will help you to do that too.

Some of the young people that I have worked with have kindly contributed their stories, thoughts and artwork to this book in order to help others learn how to control their anxiety as they have.

I hope you find this workbook fun, interesting and enjoyable as well as packed full of useful information and helpful tools to help you manage your anxiety.

Happy reading and good luck with starving your Anxiety Gremlin!

Kate

Information for Parents and Professionals

The purpose of this workbook

Starving the Anxiety Gremlin provides a cognitive behavioural approach to anxiety management for young people. It is designed for young people to work through on their own or with the support of a parent or a professional, such as a mental health practitioner, teacher, mentor, teaching assistant, social worker, doctor or youth worker. The self-help materials included in this workbook are based on the principles of cognitive behavioural therapy (CBT), but do not constitute a session by session therapeutic programme. However, the materials contained in this workbook can be used as a resource for therapists working with young people.

Please note that the My Anxiety Questionnaire in Chapter 4 is a tool for young people to use to explore and get a better understanding of their own anxiety. However, the questionnaire is not designed to be used as a clinical diagnostic tool.

Please also note that this workbook should not be considered to be a substitute for professional treatment where required.

What is cognitive behavioural therapy?

CBT is an evidence-based, skills-based, structured form of psychotherapy, which emerged from Beck's Cognitive Therapy (e.g. Beck 1976) and Ellis' Rational-Emotive Therapy (e.g. Ellis 1962), as well as from the work of behaviourists such as Pavlov (e.g. Pavlov 1927) and Skinner (e.g. Skinner 1938) on classical and operant conditioning respectively. CBT looks at the relationships between our thoughts (cognition), our feelings (emotions) and our actions (behaviours). It is based on the premise that how we interpret experiences and situations has a profound effect on our behaviours and emotions.

CBT focuses on:

- the problems that the client is experiencing in the here and now
- why the problems are occurring
- what strategies the client can use in order to address the problems.

The therapeutic process achieves this by empowering the client to identify:

- negative, unhealthy and unrealistic patterns of thoughts, perspectives and beliefs
- maladaptive and unhealthy patterns of behaviour
- the links between the problems the client is facing and his or her patterns of thoughts and behaviours
- how to challenge the existing patterns of thoughts and behaviours and implement alternative thoughts and behaviours that are constructive, healthy and realistic in order to address problems, manage emotions and improve wellbeing.

Thus the underlying ethos of CBT is that by addressing unhelpful patterns of thoughts and behaviours, people can change how they feel, how they view themselves, how they interact with others and how they approach life in general – thereby moving from an unhealthy cycle of reactions to a healthy one.

CBT has been found to be effective with a wide range of emotional wellbeing and mental health issues. For example:

- anxiety (e.g. Cartwright-Hatton *et al.* 2004 and James, Soler and Weatherall 2005)

- OCD (e.g. O'Kearney *et al.* 2006)
- depression (e.g. Klein, Jacobs and Reinecke 2007).

Furthermore, guidelines published by the National Institute for Clinical Excellence (NICE) recommends the use of CBT for a number of mental health issues, including depression (NICE 2005a) and OCD (NICE 2005b).

Although there has been less research conducted on the use of CBT with children and young people than there has been with adults, evidence for its effectiveness with children and young people is continuing to grow and being reported in a number of reviews, such as Kazdin and Weisz (1998) and Rapee *et al.* (2000). Random clinical trials have shown CBT to be effective with children and young people for:

- OCD (Barrett, Healy-Farrell and March 2004)
- depression (Lewinsohn and Clarke 1999)
- Generalised Anxiety Disorder (Kendall *et al.* 1997; 2004)
- specific phobias (Silverman *et al.* 1999)
- social phobia (Spence, Donovan and Brechman-Toussaint 2000)
- school refusal (King *et al.* 1998).

Introduction

If you have answered 'Yes' to any of the above, then *Starving the Anxiety Gremlin* is here to help you!

But please don't let the length of this workbook put you off! There are many types of anxiety and everyone's experience of anxiety is different. There are also many strategies that can help when managing anxiety and many different types of activities that you can complete to help you practise the anxiety management skills that you learn. So I have tried to cover as much about anxiety and anxiety management as possible. As a result, working through this whole book will give you the fullest knowledge and the most practice opportunities. But, if you want to make a quick start please feel free to dip in and out of the parts of the book that are most relevant to you. Don't forget you can always return to the full book at any time in the future.

Please also remember that starting to explore your anxiety may raise some difficult issues for you, so don't be afraid to talk to someone you can trust about these issues, such as a parent, relative, friend, teacher or counsellor.

So, to get you started in the process of learning to manage your anxiety, I would like to tell you one more thing about this workbook. It is based on something called cognitive behavioural therapy (CBT). CBT is where a therapist helps people to deal with a wide range of emotional problems, including anxiety, by looking at the links between how we think (our cognition), how we feel (our physical feelings and our emotions) and how we act (our behaviour).

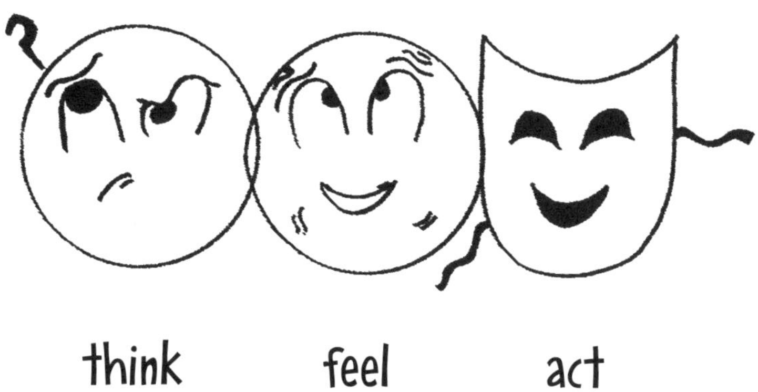

In the chapters and activities that follow, you will learn about how you:

- think
- feel (physically and emotionally)
- act.

And how this is key to understanding how to starve your Anxiety Gremlin and get your anxiety under control. So let's get started!

1

What is Anxiety?

Step 1 of managing anxiety is to understand what anxiety is.

ANXIETY is an EMOTION.

When people describe anxiety, they tend to use words like:

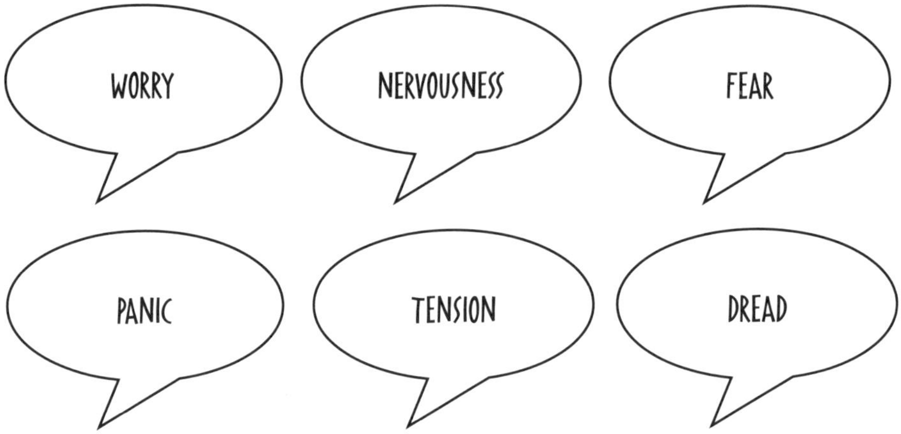

ANXIETY WORD SEARCH

See if you can find the six words above in the word search below. The answers to this word search are in the Appendix at the back of this workbook.

D	R	E	A	D	X	W	Q	R	Z	S
D	C	J	K	T	W	X	V	S	S	P
W	U	B	G	E	A	Z	A	E	M	J
O	V	H	J	N	P	M	N	W	X	O
V	T	G	U	S	J	S	K	Z	Q	B
W	Z	C	K	I	U	I	M	L	Z	A
O	X	U	S	O	M	Q	F	O	P	L
R	O	A	V	N	L	G	E	Q	D	S
R	E	R	A	Q	M	B	A	H	J	E
Y	E	C	T	Y	P	C	R	F	R	U
N	F	R	Y	P	M	P	A	N	I	C

You will see these words used throughout this workbook as they are all things that make up anxiety and they can all be normal and healthy to feel at certain times in life. For example, most people will feel *nervous* at some point in their lives, such as when taking an exam, starting a new school, performing in a school play or going on a first date. It is normal to experience nerves in situations that are new to us or that mean a lot to us. It is also normal for us to *worry* about certain things at times, such as if a loved one is ill. And it is normal to experience *fear* when faced with a dangerous or life-threatening situation. In fact, fear is important when we face dangerous situations because fear triggers a series of temporary physical changes in our bodies to help us deal with the danger ahead.

Let's get in a time machine and travel back in time to see what I mean by this...

You've stepped out of your time machine into a world where humans live in caves and sabre-tooth tigers roam the Earth. It's one million years ago. It's the Stone Age. Not too far away from you and your time machine, there's a caveman doing his normal caveman-type things, such as searching for berries to go in a caveman-sized pie for dinner! Suddenly you realise a very vicious-looking creature is stalking the caveman, preparing to pounce. Before you can shout 'It's behind you!' in true pantomime style, the caveman turns around and comes nose to nose with a sabre-tooth tiger.

What do you think the caveman is thinking right at this point? Write an example in the thought bubble coming out of the caveman's head below.

Louise, aged 13 years, wrote 'Oh noooooooooo!!' when she did this task. Carter, aged 14 years, wrote 'Run! Quick!' I'm sure you will also have written something that shows the caveman realising 'Oh no! I'm in danger. I need to survive!' Because of this thought the following things will be happening inside the caveman's body.

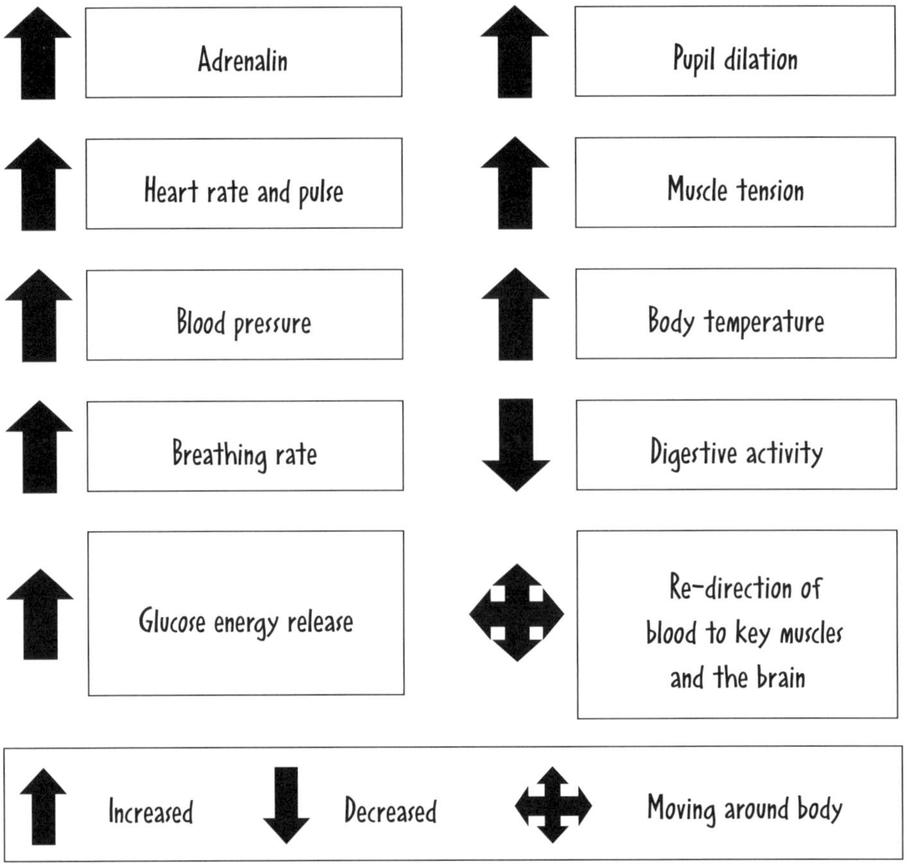

This is his body's way of preparing him to survive the life-threatening encounter with the sabre-tooth tiger or any other *real* danger that he might face in his caveman life. By making all those physical changes, his body is helping him to:

RUN FASTER	SEE AND HEAR BETTER	FIGHT HARDER
JUMP HIGHER	THINK FASTER	HEAL BETTER

OK, maybe not to the extent of your average superhero, but enough to help him have a chance of surviving that head-to-head with the tiger by either:

- defending himself through fighting back (*fight*)
- defending himself through running away to safety (*flight*)
- defending himself by playing dead so the tiger leaves him alone (*freeze*).

That is what is known as the *fight, flight or freeze response*.

So let's now whizz forward to the present day in your time machine. Let's pretend you are a scuba diver having a relaxing afternoon dive in the ocean when you suddenly realise there's a shark behind you. Write in the thought bubble below what you might be thinking.

Again, the thought will be one that highlights that you are in danger and you need to survive. It is a *real* danger and your body will trigger the very useful physical changes involved in the fight, flight or freeze response to help you deal with this emergency.

So the fight, flight or freeze response is a fantastic thing. But only if the fearful thought that triggers it is based on a *real* danger and only if this reaction calms down after the danger has passed. Thankfully, in life, real dangers very rarely occur. So these normal, occasional responses don't interfere with everyday life.

But what does this all have to do with anxiety?

Imagine you have a party to go to. Sounds simple enough, hey? But what if you start to think about all the bad things that might happen if you go to the party? What if you then start thinking that some of these bad things are really likely to happen?

Q. Are you viewing the party as safe or dangerous?

A. Dangerous, and the result is likely to be fear. Therefore your body is likely to trigger the physical changes that prepare us for a fight, flight or freeze response.

Q. But is a party a *real* danger?

A. Probably not, and if not, we are putting our body through a fight, flight or freeze false alarm and physical changes that it doesn't actually need.

If we frequently view situations or things as more dangerous than they actually are, we will keep experiencing fight, flight or freeze false alarms, just like a burglar alarm that keeps going off in response to things it shouldn't, such as thunderstorms or a passing cat! As a result, our bodies can get stuck in this fight, flight or freeze response – as though our fight, flight or freeze switch has been flicked into a permanent 'on' position.

And this state is what we call ANXIETY!

And because our bodies weren't designed to go through frequent fight, flight or freeze false alarms, this state of anxiety brings a range of negative symptoms with it. Examples can include:

COGNITIVE

Memory problems, concentration problems, obsessive thoughts, negative thoughts about yourself, unrealistic expectations of yourself, worst case scenario thoughts, 'what if?' thoughts, self-harm/suicidal thoughts, comparing self negatively to others, mind-reading thoughts, thoughts about bad things happening, blowing things out of proportion, jumping to conclusions thoughts, unrealistic thoughts about situations, 'I can't' thoughts, thoughts that focus on negatives about situations, thoughts that things are worse than they actually are, thoughts that exaggerate likelihood of danger, self-doubting thoughts, self-blaming thoughts.

PHYSICAL

Sweating, headaches, hair loss, dizziness, nausea, choking sensation, ringing in ears, red face, dry mouth, lump in throat, feeling hot, feeling cold, shortness of breath, can't catch breath, rapid breathing, heart racing, heart palpitations, chest tightness, chest pain, tingling of lips, grinding teeth, weight loss or gain, bowel problems, stomach ache or butterflies, skin problems and rashes, lack of appetite, shaking, tremors, numbness or tingling in limbs, jelly legs, fainting, tiredness, twitches or tics, muscle aches, pains and tension, frequent urination, sleep disturbance.

EMOTIONAL

Worry, feeling on edge, panic, nervousness, fear, dread, restlessness, tension, distress, upset, agitation, feeling worthless, low mood, low in confidence, low in self-esteem, feeling under pressure, feeling overwhelmed, anger, loneliness, guilt, irritability, insecurity, confusion, feeling trapped, feeling out of control, unhappiness, loss of motivation or pleasure or interest, hopelessness, numbness, hyper-sensitivity to things, self-criticism, self-doubt, defensiveness, suspiciousness, frustration.

BEHAVIOURAL

Avoidance, following rituals or routines, putting off doing things, doing things to get people's attention, seeking reassurance, checking for signs of danger, planning escape routes, binge eating, skipping meals, making yourself sick after eating, making mistakes, acting irritably, acting aggressively, sleeping more or less than usual, hiding away from people, drinking, taking drugs, self-harming, skipping school/college, ignoring problems, getting annoyed with self, getting other people to do things for you, taking out your feelings on others, bottling your anxiety up, stuttering or stammering, talking more or less or quickly, pacing, being unable to sit still, not finishing things, crying, smoking.

So now we understand what anxiety is, let's look at the different types of anxiety that can occur.

2

The Many Faces of the Anxiety Gremlin

What are Anxiety Disorders?

Anxiety can come in different shapes and sizes. Some of us get anxious in response to a wide variety of things and some of us get anxious in response to things that are more specific. Some of us also experience things called panic attacks when we get anxious. Other people feel like they have to do certain things to try and stop obsessive anxious thoughts that they have.

When a psychiatrist, psychologist, doctor or counsellor says a person has anxiety, they may say that the person has a particular type of anxiety. These professionals call these types of anxiety *anxiety disorders*.

Let's look at seven types of anxiety disorders.

1. GENERALISED ANXIETY DISORDER (GAD)

Information

Professionals describe this as intense worrying most days for at least six months.

Symptoms

When you are experiencing GAD you may:

- worry about anything and everything
- feel like you are always on edge or tense or restless
- not always understand why you feel on edge or worried
- find it hard to stop feeling like something is wrong or something bad is going to happen
- feel like the worry never goes away
- feel like the worry is taking over your life
- feel like the worry is stopping you from doing normal, everyday things
- feel unable to relax
- believe that you are unable to control how you are feeling
- experience many other symptoms, including agitation, problems sleeping, problems concentrating, tiredness, etc.

2. PANIC ATTACKS

Information

Panic attacks:

- involve an intense, overwhelming feeling of panic, anxiety, terror or fear
- last for a short period of time (normally 5 to 20 minutes)
- can occur once, occasionally or frequently
- aren't physically dangerous
- are quite common, especially in people experiencing other forms of anxiety.

Physical symptoms

These can include:

- difficulty breathing or rapid breathing
- choking sensation
- feeling faint or dizzy or legs like jelly or shaking
- heart palpitations or racing heartbeat or pains in chest
- headache
- hot or cold flush and/or sweating
- ringing in ears
- numbness or tingling in lips, fingers or toes.

Thoughts

Thoughts are usually focused on something bad happening, such as:

- 'I am losing control/I'm going crazy'.
- 'I am going to die/have a heart attack/pass out/stop breathing/choke'.

Behaviours

Feeling like you need to do certain things to avoid the impending doom that you are worried about, such as not wanting to be alone in case you pass out or escaping the situation you are in.

Panic disorder

The fear of experiencing another panic attack can often lead to:

- anxiety between attacks
- avoidance of any situations in which you have previously experienced a panic attack
- avoidance of situations where you believe you won't have access to help
- avoidance of situations where you believe that people will judge you negatively if you have a panic attack.

When this fear of panic attacks starts to occur, professionals call this panic disorder.

3. SPECIFIC PHOBIAS

Information

A phobia is when we have an exaggerated view about the level of danger that a specific situation or object may pose for us. People can experience phobias about anything. Professionals divide them into specific phobias and complex phobias. Specific phobias are a phobia about one thing. Common specific phobias include:

- animals and insects
- water
- the dark
- heights
- enclosed spaces or crowds
- injections/needles
- doctor and dentist visits
- sickness or illness
- escalators or lifts
- driving
- vomiting or vomit
- flying

- blood
- storms
- foods – including a fear of new foods.

Symptoms

- We feel intensely anxious or fearful when faced with this situation or object, but are OK when away from it.
- As a result, we tend to avoid having to face whatever we have a phobia about.
- In some cases of severe phobias, even the thought of the situation or object can trigger the phobic reaction.
- Phobias become a problem when they start having a negative or disruptive impact on you and your life.

4. COMPLEX PHOBIAS

Information

Two of the most common complex phobias are social phobia and agoraphobia.

Social phobia

Social phobia (also known as social anxiety) involves a fear of social situations, especially those involving strangers. Such situations can often include:

- parties or crowded places
- school/college lessons
- after-school/college clubs and group activities
- work-based situations that involve social interactions, such as meetings.

People with social phobia often fear:

- people observing them too closely, including other people being aware of their physical symptoms of anxiety, such as blushing, hot flushes and shaking
- other people judging them negatively or not liking them
- making a fool of themselves in front of others

- making mistakes/performing badly/standing up/speaking/eating in front of other people.

Symptoms of social phobia can include:

- predicting the worst about the social situation beforehand and viewing it as having gone badly afterwards regardless of the facts
- avoiding specific types of social situations or a wide range of social situations
- checking for physical symptoms of their anxiety that may be visible to others
- withdrawing from other people in social situations, such as hiding in a corner or avoiding speaking to people or avoiding talking about him/herself
- avoiding eye contact or speaking quietly or too quickly or stammering
- escaping the situation due to the level of anxiety being experienced
- only going into social situations accompanied by someone they know.

Agoraphobia

Agoraphobia can often be described as a fear of:

- going outside
- open spaces
- leaving the person's 'comfort zone'
- leaving the person's home either at all or for long periods of time
- being alone when outside the home.

Symptoms of agoraphobia can include:

- predicting the worst about what may happen if they leave the home/go outside/enter an open space
- avoiding leaving the home/going outside/entering open spaces
- only leaving the home/going outside/entering open spaces for short periods of time or when accompanied
- panic attacks.

5. SEPARATION ANXIETY

Information

Separation anxiety can involve feeling anxious when you are away from a member of your family.

Symptoms

Symptoms can include:

- thoughts about bad things happening to family members unless they are with you
- avoiding situations that take you away from your family members (such as refusing to go to school/college)
- constantly checking on your family members when they are away from you (such as texting or phoning family members a lot)
- not wanting to go to sleep alone.

6. HEALTH ANXIETY

Information

When someone has health anxiety, they worry about their health to an excessive level a lot of the time and when there is no medical reason to do so.

Thoughts

These can include:

- predicting the worst about your health
- not being able to get rid of thoughts about illness
- focusing obsessively on your body and any potential symptoms
- thinking that signs of illness could have been missed
- worrying about dying.

Behaviours

These can include:

- seeking reassurance from family members, friends and professionals
- frequently checking your body for potential symptoms of ill health
- seeking out or avoiding information on illnesses
- acting as though you are ill, for example, staying off school/college, staying at home.

7. OBSESSIVE COMPULSIVE DISORDER (OCD)

Information

We can all experience obsessive thoughts or a compulsive need to do things (e.g. check something) at certain times in our lives. However, these become a problem when they develop into a major part of your everyday life and when they are having a negative impact on you. This is what is known as OCD.

Symptoms

When someone experiences OCD they can have obsessions or both obsessions and compulsions.

Obsessions are repetitive, intrusive, unwanted thoughts or images that can result in unrealistic fears and a high level of anxiety. Common obsessions include thoughts:

- about death or harm to you or others
- about illness, disease, germs or contamination
- about something bad happening
- about causing harm to others or having caused or failed to prevent harm

- that certain numbers are lucky or unlucky
- that are distressed in response to things in life not being ordered/organised.

Compulsions are acts or rituals that the person feels they have to do otherwise something bad will happen. Some of these compulsions will be linked to the obsessive thoughts that the person has, for example, compulsive hand-washing in response to obsessive thoughts about germs. Compulsion examples include excessive:

- hand-washing/cleaning
- counting
- repeating tasks a certain number of times, such as repeating certain words or prayers or repeatedly touching things or repeatedly checking things
- organising/ordering/arranging things
- measuring
- hoarding
- seeking reassurance
- avoidance
- compulsively thinking about a certain phrase, word or image.

ANXIETY DISORDERS CROSSWORD

So let's have a look at what you've learnt about anxiety disorders by having a go at the crossword below.

CLUES

ACROSS

1. A complex phobia where people are afraid of leaving their house.

8. _ _ _ _ _ _ _ _ _ _ _ _ _ anxiety is a type of anxiety where you are afraid of leaving your family and what might happen to them if you are not with them.

9. _ _ _ _ _ _ _ anxiety is a type of anxiety where you worry about illness.

10. See 4 down.

12. See 4 down.

DOWN

2. _ _ _ _ _ _ _ _ _ _ _ _ _ anxiety disorder is when a person worries most of the time about most things.

3. See 7 down.

4. and 12 across and 10 across. What does OCD stand for? (9, 10, 8)

5. What type of Gremlin do you need to starve?

6. A _ _ _ _ _ _ _ _ _ phobia is a type of anxiety disorder that involves being afraid of one thing or situation.

7. and 3 down. When someone has an intense feeling of anxiety out of the blue that lasts for up to 20 minutes they are having a _ _ _ _ _ _ _ _ _ _ _ _ _ _ (5, 6)

11. _ _ _ _ _ _ _ phobia is when someone is anxious about situations that involve being around, having conversations with and standing up in front of other people.

You can find the answers to this crossword in the Appendix.

Don't be disheartened if any of the descriptions you have read in this chapter sound like you. This book is here to help you get your anxiety under control. So let's continue!

3

You're not On Your Own

Anxiety in Other Young People

The research

Step 2 of managing anxiety is realising that you are not on your own in experiencing anxiety.

You have probably had a go at doing your own research project on a particular topic at school or college. Maybe you came up with a list of questions to ask people in face-to-face interviews. Maybe you designed a survey questionnaire for people to fill out. People called researchers have asked children and young people about anxiety and the things they get anxious about using these same research methods. Let's take a look at some examples of what research has found.

A UK Office of National Statistics Child and Adolescent Mental Health survey (Green *et al.* 2005) found that:

- 2.2 per cent of 5 to 10-year-olds have an anxiety disorder.
- 4.4 per cent of 11 to 16-year-olds have an anxiety disorder.

A UK office of National Statistics survey (Singleton *et al.* 2001) found that:

- 1.4 per cent of 16 to 19 year olds have generalised anxiety disorder.

A study conducted in 2003 by the NSPCC (NSPCC 2004) of 11 to 16-year-olds and parents of 11 to 16-year-olds in England, Wales and Northern Ireland found that:

- 34 per cent of young people studied felt that they were always worrying about something.
- 11 per cent of young people were extremely worried.

- The same NSPCC study found that the things that the young people worried about most were:
  - exams
  - falling out with friends
  - having too much homework
  - the health of their family
  - being attacked on the street
  - their health
  - their appearance
  - not having enough money to do the things they want
  - arguments with parents
  - death
  - people they knew taking drugs
  - other people expecting them to try things that they don't want to do.

The NSPCC study (NSPCC 2004) also found that of the young people surveyed:

- 40 per cent talked to their parents about their worries.
- Girls were more likely to talk to their mums and boys to their dads.
- When asked to choose between a list of who they would talk to about their worries, mums came top, followed by friends. Teachers were the least likely to be talked to.

- Reasons given by the young people in the same NSPCC study for not talking to their parents about their worries included:
  - their parents didn't understand what they had to cope with.
  - their parents would over-react
  - they would worry or upset their parents
  - they would be told off
  - they would be made to feel stupid
  - they would not be believed.
- When asked what would make them want to discuss their worries with someone, the reasons included:
  - being listened to
  - if the person had experienced the same thing
  - being believed
  - if the person knew how to sort out the problem
  - not being judged
  - keeping it confidential
  - not being told off
  - if the person didn't try to take control.

You have just read what research has found out about children and young people and anxiety. Now it's your chance to think about what you think is important to ask young people about anxiety.

YOUNG, FAMOUS AND POSSIBLY ANXIOUS

If you were going to interview a famous young person about anxiety, which of the following would you choose to be?

TV CHAT SHOW HOST

☐

RADIO DJ

☐

NEWSPAPER JOURNALIST

☐

Write down the names of three famous young people that you would like to interview about anxiety.

1. ....

2. ....

3. ....

Write down three questions that you would like to ask the famous young people about anxiety.

1. ....

2. ....

3. ....

Now let's have a look at some stories from other young people about their anxiety.

'I worry about things all the time. I can worry about anything. I wish I could stop as it's ruining my life.' (Vicky, 13)

'I worry a lot about what other people think of me. I don't like how I look. I think I'm ugly and I worry that other people will laugh at me if I go out to parties.' (Steph, 16)

'I can't get thoughts of bad things happening out of my head. I can't say certain numbers as I worry that if I do something bad will happen. And I worry that something bad will happen if I don't have things in a specific order in my bedroom and if I don't get ready for school using the same routine every day.' (Steven, 11)

'I feel so sick when I'm anxious that I can't eat. I also find it hard to concentrate in lessons at school if something is worrying me. I worry a lot about problems between my mum and dad at home. I worry that they might get divorced and that it might be my fault as they argue a lot about me.' (Paul, 12)

'I believe I should be perfect and I get so anxious about not doing things perfectly. I know people won't like me if I'm not perfect.' (Hayley, 17)

'I worry a lot about my mum or dad getting ill or something else bad happening to them. I also worry about bad things that I hear about on TV. Some nights I can't get to sleep because of all the bad thoughts going round and round in my head.' (Melanie, 10)

'I find it difficult to talk in front of other people. It makes me really anxious. I start to shake and stutter and I feel like my heart is going to explode out of my chest.' (Wes, 15)

'I'm fed up of having panic attacks. I feel like I can't breathe. I get so scared and I'm sure I'm going to stop breathing completely when I have an attack. They used to just happen without me knowing why, but now I have them because I worry about going to certain places as I've had panic attacks in those places before.' (Katie, 14)

Do any of these stories sound familiar? Don't worry if they do as you can bring your anxiety under control just like the young people who shared their stories did! Step 3 in this process is to learn more about your own anxiety. So let's get started on this by completing the My Anxiety Questionnaire.

4

My Anxiety

MY ANXIETY QUESTIONNAIRE

1. How often do you feel anxious? Tick which answer applies to you.

a) Most of the time ☐

b) Often ☐

c) Sometimes ☐

d) Rarely ☐

e) Never ☐

2. How long have you been experiencing anxiety for? Tick which answer applies to you.

a) For as long as I can remember ☐

b) For years ☐

c) For months ☐

d) For weeks ☐

3. Think about how you tend to feel physically when you get anxious. Highlight or colour in any of the following that apply to you.

- TINGLING OR NUMB LIPS
- HEADACHES
- HAIR LOSS
- DIZZINESS
- RED FACE
- CHOKING SENSATION
- DRY MOUTH
- LUMP IN THROAT
- RINGING IN EARS
- GRINDING TEETH
- HEART RACING OR PALPITATIONS
- RAPID OR SHALLOW BREATHING
- CHEST TIGHTNESS OR PAIN
- SHORTNESS OF BREATH OR CAN'T CATCH BREATH
- STOMACH ACHE OR BUTTERFLIES
- NAUSEA
- SKIN PROBLEMS
- WEIGHT LOSS OR GAIN
- BOWEL PROBLEMS
- LACK OF APPETITE
- FREQUENT URINATION
- SHAKING OR TREMORS
- HOT
- TIREDNESS
- COLD
- SLEEP DISTURBANCE
- JELLY LEGS
- FAINTING
- SWEATING
- TWITCHES OR TICS
- MUSCLE PAIN, ACHE OR TENSION
- NUMBNESS OR TINGLING IN LIMBS

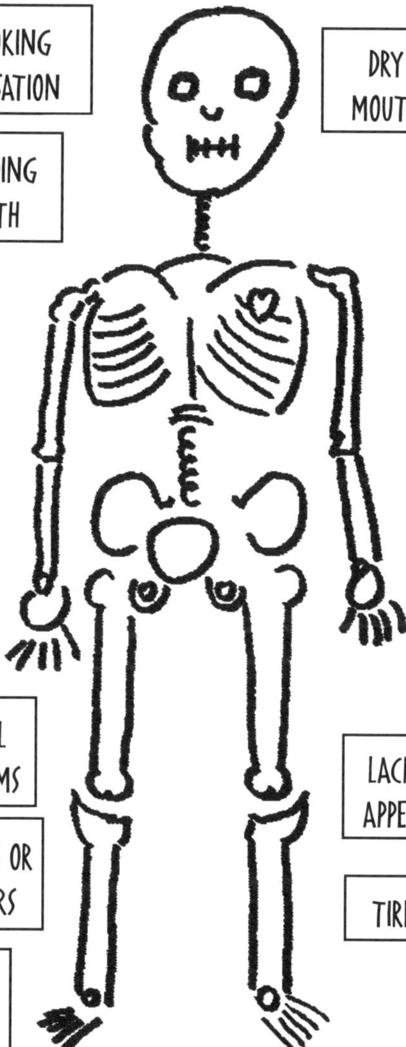

4. Rate the following possible sources of anxiety on a scale of 0 to 10.

0 = You experience no anxiety in response to that source.

10 = You experience a high level of anxiety in response to that source.

POTENTIAL SOURCE	RATING	POTENTIAL SOURCE	RATING
School/college		Work	
Family		Friendships	
Leaving the house		Enclosed spaces	
Untidiness		Germs/ contamination	
Boyfriend/girlfriend		Others' expectations of you	
Performing/ speaking in groups		Travelling by car/bus/train/ plane/boat	
Bullying		Change	
Animals/ insects/birds		The dark	
Expectations of self		Peer pressure	
Social situations		Crowded places	
The future		Your health	
How you look		Being perfect	
Health of others		Actions of others	

POTENTIAL SOURCE	RATING	POTENTIAL SOURCE	RATING
Problems at home		Living environment	
Crime and safety		Attitudes of others	
Parties		Public places	
Storms		Injections/needles	
Being away from family		Harm to others	
What other people think of you		How well you achieve at things in life	
Your responsibilities		The media	
Things being unlucky		Fire	
Getting into trouble		Worrying about worrying	
Using the telephone		Being alone	
Heights		Food	
World news		Exams	
Blood		Things going wrong	
Death		Visiting doctor or dentist	
Water		Speaking to people	

5. **Do you ever act in any of the following ways when you get anxious? Tick any that apply.**

- ☐ Avoid things
- ☐ Self-harm
- ☐ Do things to get people's attention
- ☐ Seek reassurance from others
- ☐ Avoid leaving the house
- ☐ Put off doing things
- ☐ Hide away from people, such as friends or family
- ☐ Deny you have a problem
- ☐ Check for signs of danger
- ☐ Binge eat
- ☐ Drink excessively
- ☐ Get other people to do things for you
- ☐ Skip meals
- ☐ Plan escape routes out of places or situations
- ☐ Act irritably towards people
- ☐ Make mistakes
- ☐ Only go out if accompanied
- ☐ Skip school/college
- ☐ Cry
- ☐ Act aggressively
- ☐ Check yourself for physical signs of anxiety or illness
- ☐ Stay in bed
- ☐ Ignore problems
- ☐ Take drugs
- ☐ Get annoyed with self
- ☐ Make yourself sick after eating
- ☐ Leave situations
- ☐ Follow rituals or routines obsessively

6. **Are there any other ways that you tend to act when anxious that aren't on the previous list? If so, write them down here.**

....

....

....

7. **Do any of the following thought patterns apply to you when you are anxious? Highlight or colour in any that apply.**

'WHAT IF?' THOUGHTS	NEGATIVE THOUGHTS ABOUT YOURSELF	THOUGHTS ABOUT WORST CASE SCENARIOS
'I CAN'T' THOUGHTS	UNREALISTIC EXPECTATIONS OF YOURSELF	THOUGHTS ABOUT HARMING YOURSELF
THOUGHTS WHERE YOU JUMP TO CONCLUSIONS	THINKING THAT THINGS ARE WORSE THAN THEY ACTUALLY ARE	
UNREALISTIC THOUGHTS ABOUT SITUATIONS	THINKING THAT THINGS WILL BE WORSE THAN THEY ARE LIKELY TO BE	
FOCUSING ON NEGATIVES ABOUT SITUATIONS	OBSESSIVE THOUGHTS	THOUGHTS THAT EXAGGERATE BADNESS
THOUGHTS WHERE YOU BLOW THINGS OUT OF PROPORTION	THOUGHTS THAT EXAGGERATE DANGER	SELF-BLAMING THOUGHTS
THOUGHTS THAT EXAGGERATE LIKELIHOOD OF THINGS HAPPENING	THOUGHTS WHERE YOU COMPARE YOURSELF NEGATIVELY TO OTHERS	
PREDICTING WHAT OTHER PEOPLE ARE THINKING	SELF-DOUBTING THOUGHTS	OVER-GENERALISING THOUGHTS

8. How often do you experience panic attacks when anxious? Tick which answer applies to you.

a) Often ☐ c) Rarely ☐

b) Sometimes ☐ d) Never ☐

9. Do you ever find it harder to remember things or concentrate on things when you are anxious? Circle your answer.

a) Yes b) No

10. Which of the following words do you associate with your anxiety? Highlight or colour in any that apply to you.

WORRIED	ON EDGE	PANICKY
NERVOUS	AFRAID	TRAPPED
FULL OF DREAD	RESTLESS	TENSE

11. Do you ever feel any of the following as a result of your anxiety? Highlight or colour in any that apply to you.

UPSET

WORTHLESS

AGITATED

SUSPICIOUS OF OTHERS

UNDER PRESSURE

LONELY

GUILTY

ASHAMED

LOW IN CONFIDENCE

OVERWHELMED

IRRITABLE

LOW IN MOOD

ANGRY

CONFUSED

OUT OF CONTROL

DEFENSIVE

INSECURE

STRESSED

LIKE A FAILURE

UNHAPPY

EMBARRASSED

12. Does your anxiety have any negative effects on any of the following aspects of your life? Highlight or colour in any that apply.

Physical health	Mental health and emotional wellbeing
Family relationships	Friendships
Performance at school/college/work/leisure activities	
Motivation to do things	Romantic relationships

13. Do you believe your anxiety is in or out of your control? Circle your answer.

a) In my control   b) Out of my control

If the questionnaire revealed that you experience a lot of anxiety and a lot of negative symptoms and impacts, please don't worry. Remember, understanding your own anxiety better is the third step to managing your anxiety.

So, why not have a go at another activity that can help you to understand what anxiety looks like for you, but this time in a more creative way. In the next Anxiety Box, try doing one of the following:

- Draw a picture of what your anxiety is like.
- Write a song/rap about your anxiety.
- Write a poem about your anxiety.
- Write a short story/play about your anxiety.
- Write a blog about your anxiety.
- Take a photo/series of photos that represent your anxiety.
- Draw/write down ideas for a short film about your anxiety.
- Draw/write down ideas for a dance piece about your anxiety.

To inspire you, you'll find a poem that Michelle, aged 15 years, wrote about her anxiety and some pictures created by other young people on page 56.

ANXIETY BOX

Let's get creative

The Anxiety Within

At the break of day
When everything should be OK
I can't leave my bed
Because my body's so full of dread

It's hard to explain
Without using words like pain
It's too hard to express
Without causing me so much distress

It's with me every day
No matter what I do or say
It's always inside me
They call it my anxiety

I want to get rid
It's haunted me since I was a kid
I so want to be free
Of my so-called anxiety

'My Anxiety' by Craig, 10

'My Anxiety' by Mollie, 14

'My Anxiety' by Simon, 16

You've now learnt what your anxiety looks like and that you're not on your own in feeling anxious, so now let's introduce an annoying creature called the Anxiety Gremlin!

5

The Anxiety Gremlin

How Anxiety Occurs

Understanding how anxiety occurs is Step 4 in managing anxiety.

In the previous chapter, you rated how anxious you felt in response to lots of possible sources of anxiety. Another word for these possible anxiety sources is *triggers*. These triggers can be:

- PEOPLE
- PLACES
- SITUATIONS
- THINGS ABOUT YOU
- ACTIONS
- ATTITUDES
- OBJECTS

In the Anxiety Box below, write down a list of your anxiety triggers.

ANXIETY BOX

My anxiety triggers

You will probably have realised by now that we are all different when it comes to what we worry about. What one person finds worrying, another person can see as a positive challenge or as something exciting. As a result, not everyone will experience chronic anxiety or an anxiety disorder. As we said in Chapter 2, of those of us that do experience anxiety, some of us will get anxious in response to a wide variety of things and some of us will get anxious in response to things that are more specific. We are all different.

So what leads to these differences? What causes one person to experience anxiety in a certain situation and another person not to? To answer that question, let's meet the Anxiety Gremlin.

The Anxiety Gremlin Model

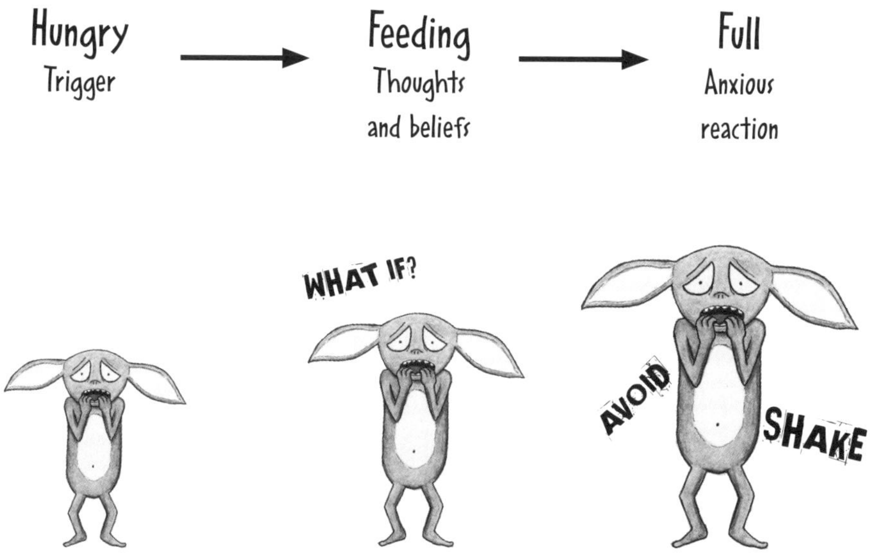

Situations, places, objects, people and their actions and attitudes are all *triggers* that are often believed to *cause* anxiety or *make us* anxious, as though we have no control over whether we get anxious or not. Well, this is what the Anxiety Gremlin wants you to think!

But if this was really the case, what would be the point in trying to control our anxiety? We would just be puppets on a very anxious string! And guess who'd be holding the puppet strings...your Anxiety Gremlin!

Thankfully, as the Anxiety Gremlin Model shows, situations *don't* make us anxious. They are only ever *triggers*. Think about it! If it was a situation that caused us anxiety, we would all feel and react in the same ways in the same situations. But we don't. As the Anxiety Gremlin Model shows, it is how we *think* about a situation that leads to our anxiety. It is how we *think* about the situation that *feeds* our *Anxiety Gremlin*, making him bigger and bigger and fuller and fuller!

Let's look at an example scenario that highlights this.

THREE FRIENDS AND A GEOGRAPHY PRESENTATION!

Three friends, Freddie, Matthew and Grace, aged 11, have to write and give a presentation in geography about volcanos. They each have to write their presentation at home and then deliver it in the following week's geography lesson. This is the first time any of them have done a presentation.

Freddie

Freddie's dad has always talked about finding presentations at work very difficult. He's often spoken to Freddie about how horrible it is to stand up in front of other people and talk. Freddie starts to think about all the possible horrible feelings he might have when he gives his presentation. He starts to avoid eating as he feels sick and begins to plan a variety of ways to get out of doing the presentation as he is so worried about not being able to cope with the horrible feelings that he is expecting it to cause. He eventually decides to tell his geography teacher that his presentation was accidentally deleted from his home computer.

Matthew

Matthew knows he isn't the best person at reading out loud. But he keeps telling himself that he can do it and that he just has to practise as much as he can beforehand so that he will feel more comfortable. He talks about it with his mum and she listens to him rehearse. She tells him how good his presentation sounds and he feels happy. The night before the presentation he keeps thinking 'I just have to try my best and so what if it doesn't go brilliantly, it's not the end of the world. The most important thing is that I try.' On the day of the presentation Matthew feels nervous and has butterflies in his stomach, but keeps thinking positive thoughts.

Grace

Grace doesn't like standing up in front of other people. The thought of people looking at her makes her anxious. She also worries that people will judge her negatively and that she will make a fool of herself. At the age of nine, she had experienced a panic attack while speaking in a class assembly. Nowadays, Grace comes up with as many ways as she can to avoid situations that involve her speaking or standing up in front of others. The moment she hears about the geography presentation, she immediately starts to think negatively about the situation and about herself. 'I'm rubbish at these things. I will make a fool of myself. People will think I'm stupid and say nasty things about me.' She feels like she can't breathe and she starts to shake. She decides that the only way forward is to pretend to be ill on the day of the presentation and not go to school.

Q. Each of the three friends is facing the same situation – giving a presentation. But do they each react in the same way? Circle your answer.

Yes No

Q. Which of the three friends seems to be the least anxious? Circle your answer.

Freddie Matthew Grace

Q. Why do you think this person ends up being less anxious about the presentation than their friends?

....

....

Q. Which friends are feeding their Anxiety Gremlin?

....

....

Well done if you have written that:

- Each of the friends reacts in a different way to the same situation.
- Matthew appears to be less anxious than Freddie and Grace.
- Freddie and Grace are feeding their Anxiety Gremlins.

Matthew is less anxious because he *thinks* in a different way about the situation and his ability to cope with it than Freddie and Grace do. Freddie and Grace think negatively about the situation whereas Matthew thinks realistically about it and tries to focus on positive ways forward. And because he *thinks* differently about the situation he then...

FEELS DIFFERENTLY PHYSICALLY	FEELS DIFFERENTLY EMOTIONALLY	BEHAVES DIFFERENTLY
For example: normal nervous butterflies.	For example: calmer.	For example: does positive things to prepare for the presentation.

Let's look at this using something called the Anxiety Gremlin Cycle.

The Anxiety Gremlin Cycle

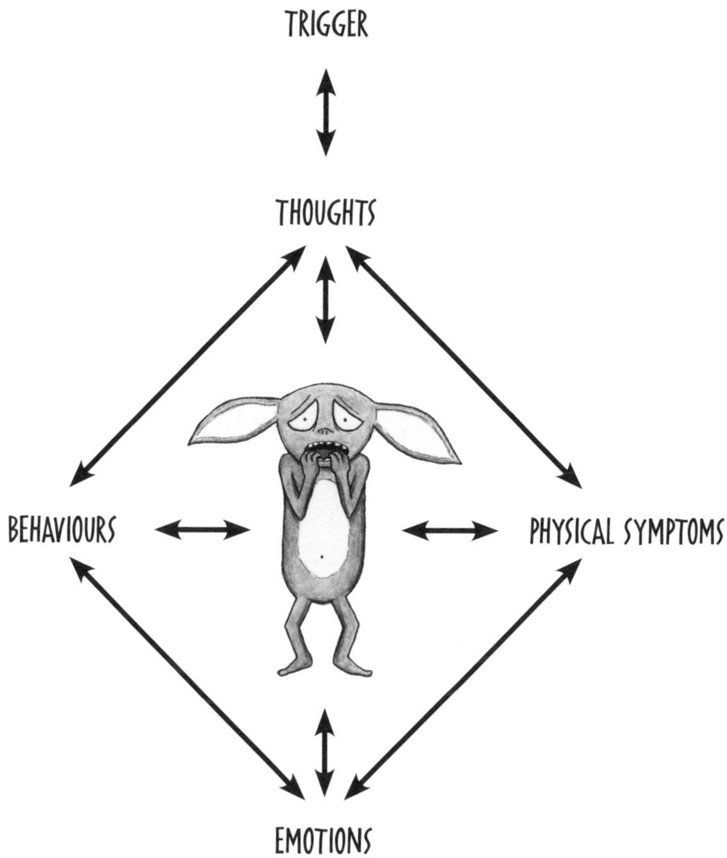

The Anxiety Gremlin Cycle shows the links between our thoughts, feelings and behaviours when we get anxious, and is based on a cognitive behavioural approach. It highlights how anxiety is maintained due to an interaction between:

- THE TRIGGER
- OUR THOUGHTS
- OUR PHYSICAL SYMPTOMS

- **OUR BEHAVIOURAL REACTION**
- **OUR EMOTIONAL REACTION.**

The Anxiety Gremlin Cycle shows:

- If we think about a particular situation we are facing in a negative and out of proportion way, we feed our Anxiety Gremlin.
- The more we feed our Anxiety Gremlin, the more anxious physical symptoms we are likely to experience.
- The more we think in a negative or out of proportion way and the more anxious physical symptoms we experience, the more likely it is that our behaviours will become unconstructive.
- The more unconstructive our behaviours, the more we feed our Anxiety Gremlin and the more negative or out of proportion our thoughts will get and the more anxious physical symptoms we will experience.
- The result – we end up stuck in the middle of a vicious cycle of anxiety, where our Anxiety Gremlins get bigger and bigger and fuller and fuller and we get more and more anxious!
- We might also start to experience other negative emotions, such as stress or low mood, thus bringing other Gremlins along to keep our Anxiety Gremlins company!

So it is how we *think* about a *situation* that affects how we then feel both *emotionally* and *physically* and how we then choose to *behave*. Let's look at two examples to show what I mean by this.

EXAMPLE 1

If we think we are going to die when we have a panic attack, we are more likely to keep that panic attack and its physical symptoms going. Thus we are feeding our Anxiety Gremlin. And if we start believing that we will have a panic attack again and that it will be really horrible and scary, we are more likely to keep our anxiety going between panic attacks – again feeding that hungry Gremlin! Plus, if we start to avoid certain situations out of a fear of having a panic attack, we don't get the chance to see that it will all be OK and once again we feed our Gremlin and keep the anxiety going.

EXAMPLE 2

If we have obsessive thoughts that we are going to be contaminated by the germs of others and that something very bad will happen to us as a result, we are going to feel anxious. If we feel the only way to stop this happening is to wash our hands over and over again every day and to clean our house several times a day, we are feeding our Anxiety Gremlin and keeping those thoughts going. This is because we don't give ourselves the opportunity to see that if we don't wash our hands that many times each day, we will still be OK. Instead we are more likely to think that the hand-washing is the only way to protect ourselves. We may then start to avoid situations where we come into contact with other people as our level of anxiety increases, which will feed our Anxiety Gremlins some more and will once again get us caught in a vicious cycle of anxiety.

But if these examples sound familiar all is not lost as Step 5 in managing your anxiety is recognising the following:

- The situation is only the trigger and **YOU** have a *choice* as to how you react to that trigger.
- **YOU** can *choose* to *think* differently.
- **YOU** can *choose* to *act* differently.
- **YOU** are in *control* of your reactions.
- **YOU** are in *control* of your *Anxiety Gremlin*.

Why not have a go at drawing your own Anxiety Gremlin in the Anxiety Box given on the next page. Then give your Anxiety Gremlin a name!

ANXIETY BOX

My Anxiety Gremlin named ....

So now let's look at Step 6 in managing your anxiety – understanding the effects anxiety can have on our lives.

6

Effects of Anxiety

Anxiety can have consequences for all of us. Think about your experiences of anxiety and feeding your Anxiety Gremlin. Write in the box below how you think your anxiety has affected you and your life.

ANXIETY BOX

Effects of my anxiety on me

Here are some stories from other young people about how their anxiety has affected them.

> 'My OCD makes me feel so ashamed of myself and so guilty, as I have such bad thoughts. I would never act on the thoughts, but I still feel like a bad person for having them.' (Tim, 13)

> 'I have avoided doing so many things because of my panic attacks. I was so worried about having more panic attacks that I stopped attending my college lessons in case I had one there. I've missed out on so much because of this.' (Mandy, 17)

> 'I have lost lots of friends as I stopped going out as it made me so worried. In the end, I just stopped leaving the house completely. I barely even speak to my friends on the phone now as I'm afraid of what they think of me.' (Alanis, 14)

> 'I have really bad dreams due to my anxiety. But that's when I can even get to sleep in the first place as I find it so hard to sleep with thoughts whizzing around my head. I wake up with a panic attack sometimes too. It's all making me really tired, which is also making me really irritable and low in mood.' (Tess, 10)

> 'I got so anxious every time I had to go out in public because of a fear of what people would be thinking about me and because I kept worrying that horrible things would happen that in the end I stopped going to school or going out with friends. I only ever see my grandma if she visits me at home. My school is trying to help me get back to school, but I'm worried about returning. But if I don't, I'm going to get even more behind at school. I keep thinking that if I don't pass my exams I won't get a job, but then I don't know how I'd cope with a job anyway. I'm so fed up of being me.' (Lauren, 15)

'I was sick several years ago and since then I have been so worried about the illness coming back again. I started checking myself every day for signs that it might be back and I kept reading about the illness on the internet. After a while, I started reading about lots of other illnesses and I now worry about getting all of them. I just can't cope anymore. It's taken over my life.' (Leah, 16)

'I have no confidence in myself anymore as I worry so much about everything. I think I'm useless and a waste of space. I even worry about worrying.' (Shane, 12)

'I have so many routines that I have to follow so that the bad things I worry about won't happen. I end up having no time left to do fun things and my friends think I'm crazy.' (Mitch, 11)

Our anxiety can also have impacts on other people around us. Again, think about times when you have been anxious. Write down what impacts you think your anxiety has had on others in the box that follows.

ANXIETY BOX

Effects of my anxiety on others

Here are some stories from other young people about how their anxiety has affected other people around them.

'My mum got into trouble with the school and social services because I kept skipping school due to my anxiety. Eventually, they all realised what was going on and I've got the help I needed, but it was really hard on my mum for a long time.' (Beth, 14)

'I started self-harming to try and calm down my anxiety and block it out. My parents have just found out and I can tell they are so disappointed in me. My mum keeps crying. I feel so bad. It's made things worse for everyone.' (David, 16)

'I worry so much about bad things happening to my mum and dad when I'm away from them. I often get so distressed in a morning about the thought of leaving them to go to school, that I don't go. My mum has had a lot of time off work as a result. My mum and dad very rarely get to go out on their own, and when they do, I'm phoning them all the time. I also won't go to sleep unless my mum is in the room with me. It's putting a strain on all of us.' (Mia, 12)

'My OCD puts a lot of stress on everyone else in the house as it takes me so long to leave the house every morning. I make my brothers late for school and my dad late for work. Sometimes I make my dad turn back round to check the doors one more time or to check the oven is off and things like that. My dad tries to be understanding, but he gets angry and upset a lot.' (Michael, 11)

So as you can see, when we are experiencing anxiety frequently, intensely or over a long period of time it can have a negative impact on us and others. This can include affecting:

PHYSICAL HEALTH

FOR YOU – examples could include making you more likely to get illnesses, making current illnesses worse, and making pain levels worse.

FOR OTHERS – worrying about your anxiety can impact on the physical health of others around you in a variety of ways.

MENTAL AND EMOTIONAL HEALTH

FOR YOU – anxiety can often lead to other emotional issues, such as stress or low mood, as well as low self-esteem, confidence and assertiveness levels. Anxiety can also impact upon our happiness levels and life satisfaction in general.

FOR OTHERS – your anxiety can impact on the emotional wellbeing of others, such as your parents who may worry a lot about you.

RELATIONSHIPS

FOR YOU AND OTHERS – the way you react when you get anxious can have an impact on your relationships with others, especially if you withdraw from others when anxious or get irritable with people.

PERFORMANCE, MOTIVATION AND FUN!

FOR YOU – your anxiety can have a negative impact on your ability to perform well at things, your ability to achieve your goals and ambitions for the future, and it can impact on you leading a full and active life.

FOR OTHERS – your anxiety can also have an impact on the lives of others in similar ways, such as their performance at work or their social lives.

Let's look at one more story that highlights the short- and long-term effects of anxiety and how one person's life can be affected in so many different ways.

MELISSA'S WORLD

Melissa is 15 years old. When she was six years old she vomited in front of everyone at a friend's birthday party. Ever since, Melissa has been afraid of being sick. The thought of being sick makes her heart race, her hands and legs shake and her head pound. Also, the more she thinks about being sick, the more she actually feels sick.

Whenever Melissa goes anywhere in public she worries about the possibility that she might be sick in front of other people and that she won't make it to a bathroom in time, even though she has never actually been sick since she was six years old.

After the incident when she was six years old, Melissa went to a few more birthday parties but only if her mum or dad stayed with her. However, her anxiety was so bad that in the end she stopped going to birthday parties altogether. Eventually her friends stopped inviting her to their parties. She gradually lost many of her friends as she wouldn't go out to other places with them either, such as shopping or to the cinema. She now only has one close friend left, but she only sees her at school. Her friend wants Melissa to attend a sleepover at her house. Melissa wants to go, but is worried in case she is sick when away from home.

Melissa's family like to go on long walks when they go away on holidays, but they have had to stop going as Melissa is afraid of going anywhere where there isn't a toilet nearby that she can go to if she feels sick.

Melissa has important exams next year and she is already worrying about sitting in the exam hall in case she feels sick and can't get to a toilet quickly enough. She also keeps thinking about 'what if the teacher doesn't let me go to the toilet?' She has had several panic attacks in recent months. Her sleeping is also extremely disturbed by nightmares. She is feeling less confident about taking her exams.

Melissa's mum and dad want to be able to help Melissa. They want to listen to her worries and help her to deal with them. But she refuses to talk as she is afraid of disappointing or upsetting them. They have tried to get Melissa to go to the doctor to talk about her worries, but Melissa refuses as she thinks the doctor will laugh at her.

Now you've read about Melissa, see if you can answer the following questions:

Q. What effects does Melissa's anxiety have on her physical health?

....

....

....

Q. What effects does Melissa's anxiety have on her mental health and emotional wellbeing?

....

....

....

Q. What effects does Melissa's anxiety have on her relationships?

....

....

....

Q. What effects does Melissa's anxiety have on her performance, motivation and fun?

....

....

....

Q. What thoughts are leading to Melissa's anxiety?

....

....

....

Q. Is Melissa feeding or starving her Anxiety Gremlin? Circle your answer.

Feeding Starving

The answers you have given may have included the following:

- Physical health effects: heart racing, shaking, headaches, nausea, sleep disturbance.
- Mental health and emotional wellbeing effects: anxiety, panic, lowered confidence.
- Relationships effects: losing friends, only seeing best friend when at school, not confiding in family.
- Performance, motivation and fun effects: no parties or sleepovers or outings with friends, no family holidays.
- Thoughts: what if I'm sick in front of other people? What if I'm sick when away from home? What if there isn't a toilet nearby? What if I feel sick in the exam and the teacher doesn't allow me to go to the toilet? If I talk to the doctor he will laugh at me.

Now let's look at how both you and Melissa can manage your anxiety.

7

Starving the Anxiety Gremlin

An Introduction to Anxiety Management

As I said in Chapter 1 of this workbook, occasional nerves, worry and fear are normal. We all experience them at some point in our lives. However, when we start to experience frequent anxiety that has negative impacts on us, we need to look at how to manage this.

Q. So how do we reduce such anxiety?

A. By starving our Anxiety Gremlins!

And you have already started this process by completing the following:

- Step 1 – Understanding what anxiety is.
- Step 2 – Realising you are not on your own in experiencing anxiety.
- Step 3 – Understanding more about your own anxiety.
- Step 4 – Understanding how anxiety occurs.
- Step 5 – Recognising that you are in control of your reactions.
- Step 6 – Understanding the effects anxiety can have on our lives.

All of these steps help you to start starving your Anxiety Gremlin. So what's next? To answer that question, think back to the Anxiety Gremlin Cycle again.

The Anxiety Gremlin Cycle

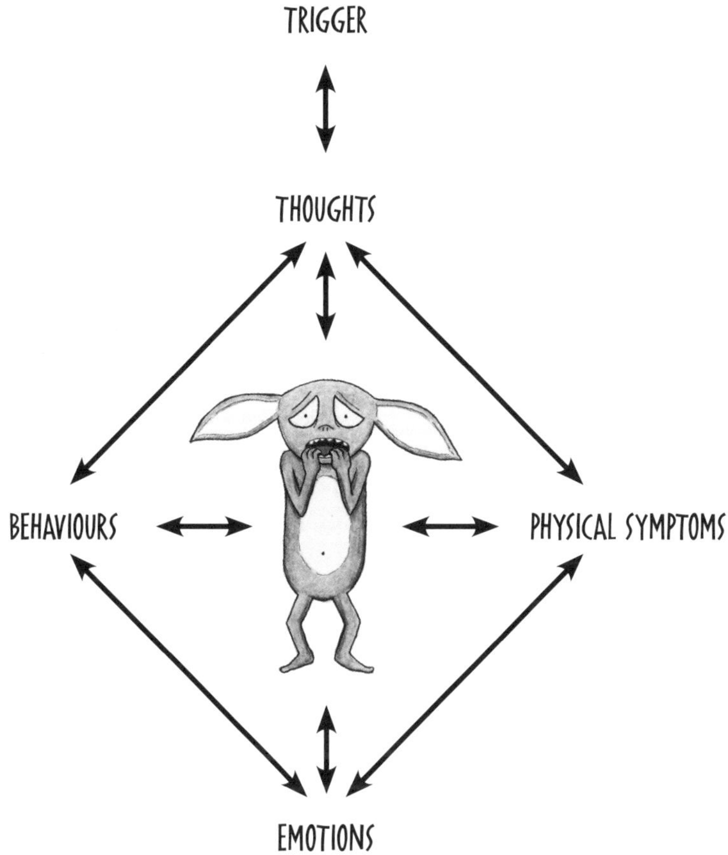

Do you remember that this cycle shows us that it is how we think and how we act that impacts on how we feel emotionally? Based on this, what do you think Steps 7 and 8 of starving your Anxiety Gremlin should be?

Yes, you've guessed it!

- Step 7 – Manage your thoughts.
- Step 8 – Manage your behaviours.

To help you understand what I mean by these, have a go at the following activity. Think about the last time you responded well to an anxiety trigger and then answer the questions in the Anxiety Box.

ANXIETY BOX

Q. What anxiety trigger did you respond well to?

....

....

....

....

Q. What were you thinking in response to the trigger?

....

....

....

....

Q. How did you act in response to the trigger?

....

....

....

....

Q. What things can you learn about anxiety management from how you handled this situation?

....

....

....

....

....

....

....

....

....

....

We're going to look at a wide range of anxiety management strategies in the next two chapters and you may have come up with several of them in your answers to the previous activity. But first we need to be aware that there are certain things that can make some of us more susceptible to anxiety in the first place and that can therefore make it harder for us to starve our Anxiety Gremlins. However, even though certain things can sometimes make us more susceptible to experiencing anxiety, they don't stop us from being in control of our reactions (apart from in cases of severe mental illness where a person is not aware of what they are doing). We can still have an impact on our anxiety levels by looking at how we think about situations and how we choose to respond to them. We might have to work harder at starving our Anxiety Gremlins and it might take us longer to do so. But we can still do it. These factors don't have to take away our control.

For example, just because one of our parents has suffered with anxiety, it doesn't mean we have to develop it or that if we do, we can't learn to manage it. Also just because we have had anxiety in the past, it doesn't mean we have to experience it again in the future.

Let's take a look at what factors can make starving our Gremlins harder using an activity. First read through the following scenarios.

Scenario 1

Kanye is 16 years old and was diagnosed with depression at 14 years old. Due to his depression he doesn't feel motivated to go out very often. Now, whenever he has to go out somewhere, such as to the doctor to discuss his depression, he finds himself getting extremely anxious about leaving the house.

Scenario 2

Heather is 17 years old. Two years ago, her mum became very ill and was rushed to hospital. She recovered. One year ago, Heather's grandma passed away. Heather now calls her mum at least 20 times a day to check if she is OK. She struggles to get thoughts of bad things happening to the people she loves out of her head.

Scenario 3

Leon is ten years old. He had panic attacks when his parents split up. He was six years old at the time. His mum re-married when Leon was eight years old. He became very close to his step-dad. However his step-dad had an affair and has now left Leon's mum. Leon's panic attacks have returned.

Scenario 4

Penny is 14 years old and has suffered from irritability while on her periods ever since she started menstruating at the age of 12. She also gets bad period pain. Over the past year she has started having panic attacks when she is on her period.

Scenario 5

Abdul is 18 years old. Abdul's dad has suffered with OCD for as long as Abdul can remember. His dad has to check that things are switched off in the house and that the windows and doors are locked at least ten times before going to bed or leaving the house. He is also obsessive about everything having to be ordered, organised and clean and tidy. Abdul moved into a shared house at university recently and can't cope with the untidiness of his house mates. It is causing Abdul extreme levels of anxiety. He also stays up every night until all his house mates have returned home, no matter what the time, so he can check that the doors are locked.

Scenario 6

Harry is 12 years old. His dad shouts and throws things at his mum whenever he gets drunk. He also shouts at Harry when he is drunk. His dad is getting drunk most nights. Harry's mum can't afford to pay the bills and they have had debt collectors on the phone and at the door several times. Harry worries every day when he has to leave school and go home. He worries every time the phone or the doorbell rings. He worries every time his dad pours a drink. He sits in his room and cries when he hears his dad screaming and shouting. Harry doesn't know what to do to help his mum. He has nightmares about his dad's behaviour.

Scenario 7

Beth is 13 years old. She has been bullied by a group of girls at school for two years. They say horrible things about her behind her back and to her face. They post nasty things about her on social networking sites and have recently started sending her abusive text messages. Beth has heard them say so many bad things about her that she has started to believe them. She doubts herself all the time and thinks that she is useless and worthless. She calls herself stupid and ugly all the time. She believes that she isn't good at anything and gets very anxious whenever she is set an assignment or exam at school. She also thinks that no one will ever like her. She gets anxious whenever she has to meet new people or whenever she has to speak in front of other people at school as she believes she will make a fool of herself.

Scenario 8

Michael is 17 years old and started smoking cannabis 12 months ago. The amount he has been smoking has been rapidly increasing. He has noticed that the more he smokes, the more anxious he gets. He has started worrying about what other people might be thinking about him and he finds he gets very shaky and panicky.

Now think about what might have made each young person more susceptible to anxiety or what might be making it harder for them to starve their Anxiety Gremlins in each of the different scenarios that you've just read. See if you can match up the scenario number with the factor affecting the person's anxiety control in that scenario in the activity that follows. You will find the answers to this Match the Scenarios activity in the Appendix.

MATCH THE SCENARIOS

SCENARIO 1	Current experiences of multiple triggers
SCENARIO 2	Beliefs about self and the world
SCENARIO 3	Genetics or learning from other people's anxiety reactions
SCENARIO 4	Other emotional or mental health issues
SCENARIO 5	Past experiences of difficult or traumatic situations
SCENARIO 6	Past experiences of anxiety
SCENARIO 7	Physical conditions
SCENARIO 8	Drug use

Now you know what can make it harder to starve our Anxiety Gremlins sometimes, let's get started with Step 7 in the process of starving our Gremlins – managing our thoughts.

8

Starving the Anxiety Gremlin

Managing Your Thoughts

In this chapter, we will look at how you can manage your thoughts in order to starve your Anxiety Gremlin. The four strategies that I'm going to discuss are:

- thinking realistically
- recognising that your obsessive thoughts are only thoughts
- keeping your expectations of yourself realistic
- building your self-esteem, confidence and positivity.

Don't worry if it seems like there is a lot to put into practice. All four strategies can help to starve an Anxiety Gremlin, but not all of them will necessarily be relevant to you. You just need to focus on implementing those that are. Remember you can add any of the other strategies to your starving the Anxiety Gremlin armoury as and when you need to throughout life.

Thinking realistically

Do you remember learning in the previous chapters that it is how you think about a situation that determines whether you experience anxiety? This is why *thinking realistically* starves your Anxiety Gremlin.

There are four steps involved in thinking realistically as the flowchart below shows.

Mindfulness → Thought-stopping → Assessment → Challenging

MINDFULNESS

Mindfulness is being aware of how you are thinking. When you find yourself starting to feel anxious, identify what you are thinking at that point in time. Many people can find this difficult to do, often because they are so distracted by the anxious physical symptoms that they are experiencing. But it is important to work hard on trying to identify your thought patterns.

Common anxiety-related thought patterns can be divided into:

- disaster movie thinking
- thinking negatively about yourself.

Disaster movie thinking is when we predict the worst case scenario and think it is highly likely that it is going to happen. Disaster movie thinking involves expecting a disaster to be around every corner just like in a disaster movie! Examples of disaster movie thinking include:

- *Blowing things out of proportion or catastrophising* – thinking things are worse than they actually are or exaggerating danger, for example, thinking that a friend not being able to attend your birthday party is the end of the world and means they don't like you.
- *Predicting worst case scenarios* – predicting the worst possible outcome, for example, 'I am going to fail my exams no matter what I do.'
- *Jumping to negative conclusions* – such as making negative assumptions about a situation before knowing the facts, for example, 'I know I will have a panic attack if I go to the cinema tomorrow.'
- *'What if?' thinking* – worrying about what if this bad thing happens or what if that bad thing happens, without any evidence that they will happen, for example, 'What if I don't get into college? My life will be over.'
- *Exaggerating likelihood* – thinking bad things are more likely to happen than they actually are, for example, 'I'm going to get swine flu as my friend's cousin has it.'

Examples of *thinking negatively about yourself* include:

- *Putting yourself down* – focusing on your negatives and only seeing bad things about yourself, for example, 'I'm ugly and no one likes me.'
- *Blaming yourself* – thinking that everything that goes wrong is your fault, for example, 'It's my fault my parents got divorced.'
- *Having unrealistic expectations about yourself* – for example, 'I have to get top marks in all my subjects.'

- *Mind-reading* – making negative assumptions about what other people are thinking about you, for example, 'I know no one in my class likes me.'
- *'I can't' thinking* – thoughts where you doubt yourself and your abilities, for example, 'I can't stand up in front of people in the school assembly.'
- *Negative comparisons* – comparing yourself negatively to others, for example, 'All the girls in my class are prettier than me.'

In the world of CBT, these patterns of unhelpful thoughts are known as *thinking errors*.

To help you to be mindful of your thoughts, colour in or highlight which of the thinking errors in the Anxiety Box below tend to apply to your thought patterns when you are anxious?

ANXIETY BOX

WHICH THINKING ERRORS APPLY TO YOU?

PUTTING YOURSELF DOWN	NEGATIVE COMPARISONS	BLOWING THINGS OUT OF PROPORTION
EXAGGERATING THE LIKELIHOOD	HAVING UNREALISTIC EXPECTATIONS ABOUT YOURSELF	
PREDICTING WORST CASE SCENARIOS	BLAMING YOURSELF	'WHAT IF?' THINKING
JUMPING TO NEGATIVE CONCLUSIONS	'I CAN'T' THINKING	MIND-READING

THOUGHT-STOPPING

When you notice that you are thinking an anxious thought, such as a type of thought error, you can use one of the following techniques to help you to stop focusing on that thought for a moment:

- Say 'stop' or a similar word of your choice.
- Imagine a stop sign in your mind.

You can then take a deep breath and work on assessing and challenging your thought errors.

ASSESSMENT

Once you are aware of your thoughts, you need to assess them. Ask yourself questions like:

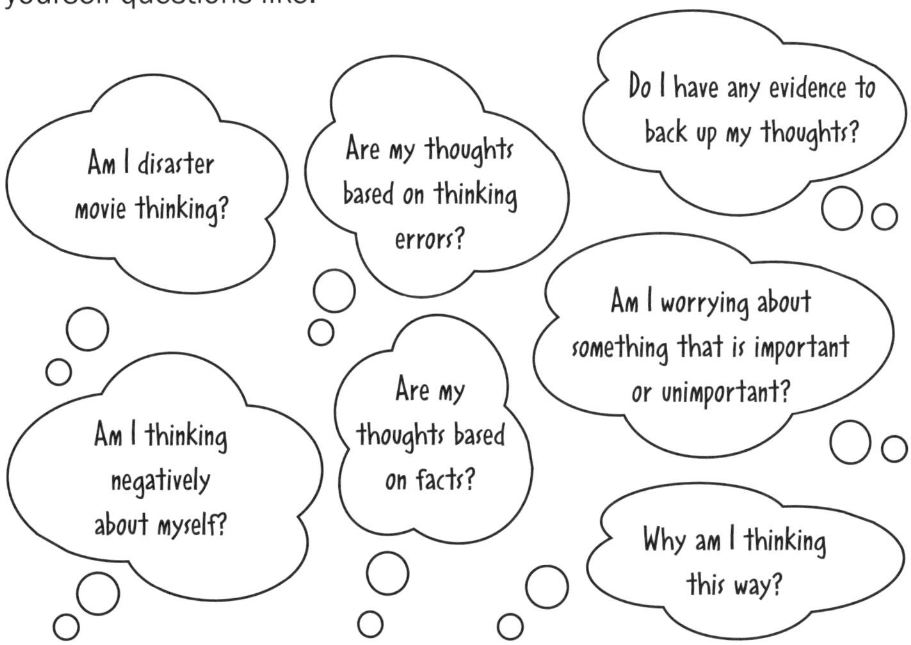

CHALLENGING

If you work out that your thoughts are out of proportion, unrealistic or negative in some way, you then need to challenge them based on realistic thinking. To do so, ask yourself questions like:

- Where will my anxiety get me?
- What is the worst thing that could happen and is it really that likely?
- What are the facts?
- If the worst thing happened would it really be that bad or would I cope somehow?
- What is a realistic way of thinking about the situation based on the facts?
- What can I do differently to deal with the situation instead of getting anxious about it?

Let's have a look at an example scenario and then have a go at answering some questions that highlight how to think realistically:

PANIC ON A BUS

Anya is 13 years old. She has had several panic attacks. Every time Anya has a panic attack she thinks that she is going to choke and die, even though this hasn't happened and her attacks calm down after about ten minutes. She also thinks that people are going to laugh at her when she struggles to breathe, but this has never happened. Anya worries about having more panic attacks in the future and is now avoiding situations that she associates with panic attacks. For example, as a result of a previous panic attack on a bus Anya won't travel by bus anymore because she thinks if she does, she will have another panic attack and die.

Q. Write down what Anya is thinking.

....

....

Q. Is Anya using any thought errors? If so, what types?

....

....

Q. Do you think Anya has any evidence to back up her thoughts? Circle your answer.

Yes No

Q. What are the facts about the situation?

....

....

Q. Do you think Anya is feeding or starving her Anxiety Gremlin? Circle your answer.

Feeding Starving

Q. How can Anya think differently?

....

....

You might have answered the above questions in a similar way to the following.

Anya's thoughts are that panic attacks are harmful and that she will choke and die. She also thinks that because she has had them before she will keep having them. She has also made links between certain situations and panic attacks, thinking that because she has had a panic attack in one situation before, she will have one in the same situation the next time. Thus, Anya is predicting the worst and exaggerating the likelihood of bad things happening. She is disaster movie thinking and she is feeding her Anxiety Gremlin.

But although panic attacks do not feel nice when they are happening, they aren't dangerous. They won't harm Anya and she won't die. She has proof of this as she has been through panic attacks in the past and she is still alive. Anya has never been laughed at during a panic attack either so again she has no evidence to support her belief that this will happen.

Anya could work on reducing her belief that something bad will happen by thinking more realistically about the situation and focusing on the facts of the situation, including that a panic attack is short and it won't harm you. She could tell herself that she has never died as a result of a panic attack and that she won't. She could also try to think more realistically about the associations she has made between situations and panic attacks, telling herself that she has no proof to support her belief that she will have a panic attack whenever she travels by bus.

Anya could also benefit from thinking more positively about her ability to cope with the situation. She has been through panic attacks before and she has coped and they have passed. She needs to remind herself of this.

So whenever you find yourself getting anxious, try to think about the situation realistically based on the facts. Make sure you aren't being overly negative in some way or blowing things out of proportion. Make sure you're not disaster movie thinking. Remember situations are normally not as bad as we think they are going to be and even if our worst case scenario actually occurs, we can normally find some way to cope with it, learn from it and move on from it. Also, instead of getting anxious about the situation, focus on what you can do to deal with it.

Some people find it easier to challenge their thoughts by writing them down, especially in the initial stages. This allows you to use these notes again in the future if you have similar thoughts. The alternative thoughts worksheet on the next two pages will help you with this and with making a start on starving your Anxiety Gremlin.

ALTERNATIVE THOUGHTS WORKSHEET

What is the trigger?

....

What are my thoughts in response to the trigger?

....

What are the facts about the situation?

....

Are my thoughts based on facts? Circle your answer.

Yes No

Am I doing any of the following?

PUTTING MYSELF DOWN	NEGATIVE COMPARISONS	HAVING UNREALISTIC EXPECTATIONS ABOUT MYSELF
EXAGGERATING THE LIKELIHOOD OF BAD THINGS HAPPENING	JUMPING TO NEGATIVE CONCLUSIONS	BLOWING THINGS OUT OF PROPORTION

PREDICTING WORST CASE SCENARIOS	MIND-READING	'WHAT IF?' THINKING	'I CAN'T' THINKING	BLAMING MYSELF

Are my thoughts feeding or starving my Anxiety Gremlin ? Circle your answer.

Feeding Starving

How can I think more realistically in order to starve my Anxiety Gremlin?

....
....
....

Recognising that your obsessive thoughts are only thoughts

This strategy is particularly appropriate for the obsessive thoughts that individuals can have when experiencing obsessive compulsive disorder (OCD).

When a person has an obsessive thought, it is only ever a thought. It does not mean that what you are thinking about over and over again will ever happen. We can all have strange thoughts at times, but they are only ever thoughts. It doesn't mean that we are ever going to act on them or that they will come true.

So keep reminding yourself that just because you are thinking something, it doesn't mean that it will happen. Accept that a thought is just a thought. This will help you to starve your Anxiety Gremlin.

If you have any obsessive thoughts, write them down in the Anxiety Box that follows and then write down a statement that you will tell yourself to help you to reduce the importance of that thought.

ANXIETY BOX

My obsessive thoughts are:

But when I have those obsessive thoughts, I will tell myself:

Keeping your expectations of yourself realistic

Expectations that you might have about yourself may include believing that you need to:

- achieve a particular thing
- act in a particular way
- be a particular type of person
- look a certain way.

Let's look at an example scenario to explore the impact that our expectations can have on us and then answer the questions that follow.

I HAVE TO BE PERFECT!

Liam is 15 years old. His parents are always talking about his older brother's achievements and how wonderful he is. Liam has grown up believing that his older brother is perfect and Liam strives to be like his brother. He studies every minute he can and gets involved with every extra-curricular activity there is at school. Liam is constantly afraid that he will make a mistake at whatever he is doing at that time. He gets mad with himself if he doesn't feel he has achieved perfection at everything. His anxiety gets particularly bad if he has an exam coming up or a school project to hand in for marking as he is afraid that he will get less than an A grade. As a result of constantly striving for perfection, Liam is extremely anxious, on edge, nervous and fearful of mistakes. His sleep is disturbed and he feels nauseous a lot of the time. He is exhausted from working so hard at everything.

Q. Do you think Liam's expectations of himself are realistic or unrealistic? Circle your answer.

Realistic Unrealistic

Q. Do you think Liam's expectations are putting too much pressure on him? Circle your answer.

Yes No

Q. What negative effects are Liam's expectations having on him?

....
....
....

Q. Do you think Liam's expectations are feeding or starving his Anxiety Gremlin? Circle your answer.

Feeding Starving

Q. How could Liam change his expectations about himself?

....
....
....

What Liam's example shows us is that if your expectations of yourself are unrealistic then you are more likely to feel anxious as you are trying to achieve things that are unachievable. Thus unrealistic expectations feed your Anxiety Gremlin!

So in order to starve your Anxiety Gremlin, remind yourself that you can only ever do your best and achieve things that are realistic for you based on your abilities, strengths and current circumstances. Also remember that no one is perfect! Perfection doesn't exist!

Think about all the expectations you place on yourself. In the Anxiety Box given, list any expectations that you place on yourself that you now realise are unrealistic and that are feeding your Anxiety Gremlin.

ANXIETY BOX

Unrealistic expectations
that I place on myself

Based on your answers to the last activity, have a go at changing your unrealistic expectations to realistic ones and write them in the Anxiety Box below. For example, Liam worked on making his expectations of himself more realistic and came up with the following expectations:

> 'I expect that I will always do the best I can.'
>
> 'I expect that I will always work as hard as I can, but not to the extent that I cause myself harm.'
>
> 'I expect that I will judge my achievements based on what I am capable of.'

ANXIETY BOX

Realistic expectations that I place on myself

Building your self-esteem, confidence and positivity

Our self-confidence and self-esteem involve:

- how much we like or approve of ourselves
- how worthy we think we are as a person.

Self-esteem and self-confidence develop based on the experiences and interactions we go through in our lives. This is because we start to develop certain ways of thinking about ourselves based on these experiences. For example, if a child is bullied, they might start to develop a belief that there is something wrong with them and that they aren't a likeable person.

People with low self-esteem will often view themselves in a negative way and, as a result, are likely to have little confidence in themselves and their abilities. If you don't believe in yourself you are less likely to think that you can cope with things that come your way and are more likely to think things will go badly, for example, thinking 'I will fail.' As a result, you are more likely to experience negative emotions, such as anxiety. So not believing in yourself can feed your Anxiety Gremlin!

Let's have a look at an example scenario that highlights this and then answer the questions that follow.

POP PRINCESSES

Two best friends, Kylie and Britney, were named after pop stars by their parents. Both are 12 years old.

Kylie

Kylie has good self-esteem. She recognises what her strengths are and what she is good at. She is happy with who she is as a person and is proud of herself. She knows she isn't good at everything in life, but doesn't expect to be. When she comes up against a situation that is difficult, she reminds herself of her positive qualities and tells herself she will cope with the situation as best she can.

Britney

Britney is lacking in confidence and self-esteem. She doesn't believe that she is good at anything and whatever situation she has to face in life, she tells herself she can't do it, that she will fail and that she will make a fool of herself.

Q. Who do you think is feeding their Anxiety Gremlin? Circle your answer.

Kylie Britney

Q. Who do you think is starving their Anxiety Gremlin? Circle your answer.

Kylie Britney

A. Kylie is starving her Anxiety Gremlin and Britney is feeding hers.

What these pop princesses show us is that in order to help starve your Anxiety Gremlin, you need to think more positively about yourself and your life, including:

Your positive characteristics	Your achievements and the positive things they show you about you

Your strengths	Things you are good at	The things that make you a likeable person

Times when you have successfully overcome difficulties and what they show you about you

Good things that happen to you every day	Positive things in your life	Positive goals for the future

Use all these things to encourage and boost you at times when you feel you're struggling, when you doubt yourself and when you feel like you can't cope with something. But remember it's not about looking at yourself through rose-tinted glasses for the sake of it. It's about looking at yourself positively based on what is factual and therefore realistic. Also remember to listen more to what you know to be true about yourself based on facts and less to others' opinions of you, unless you know they are truly valid!

These will all help to starve your Anxiety Gremlin!

Let's try some activities to start your self-esteem building process. I asked Britney from the previous example to give her answers to each of these activities too. I have given some of these to help give you inspiration for yours.

In the following Anxiety Box, list ten positive things about yourself and write down a piece of evidence to back up each statement. To give you an example of what I mean, here are two things that Britney said about herself with accompanying evidence.

> 'I am a kind person because I always do the best I can to be nice and helpful to people.'

> 'I am a good listener because I will always listen to my friends whenever they need to talk about something that is bothering them.'

ANXIETY BOX

POSITIVES ABOUT ME	THE EVIDENCE

Now list at least three things you have achieved in your life so far and write down at least one positive thing that each achievement shows you about you in the Anxiety Box below.

ANXIETY BOX

My positive achievements and what they show about me

Next write down at least five strengths that you think you have that can help you to face situations in life that normally provoke your anxiety in the Anxiety Box below.

ANXIETY BOX
My strengths

Now write down at least three things you believe you are good at in the Anxiety Box below.

ANXIETY BOX

Things I'm good at

Finally, based on everything you've come up with so far, write down five positive statements about yourself in the Anxiety Box below. We call these *positive affirmations*.

To help you with this, here are Britney's positive affirmations:

'I am a kind person.'

'I am nice to be around.'

'I am a good friend.'

'I can achieve things if I believe in myself.'

'I am proud of who I am.'

ANXIETY BOX

My positive affirmations

It can help to place the answers to all these activities somewhere where you can look at them regularly to remind yourself of all these important things about you, especially at times when you are struggling.

And remember, if you take a realistic and positive perspective, including how you view yourself and the expectations you have for yourself, coping with life events will be easier.

AND...you will be starving your Anxiety Gremlin!

OK, now let's have a look at what changes you can make to your behaviour to help you starve your Anxiety Gremlin.

9

Starving the Anxiety Gremlin

Managing Your Behaviours

I am going to list three key ways of managing your behaviour in order to starve your Anxiety Gremlin. These areas are:

- reducing your reliance on safety behaviours
- reducing compulsive behaviours
- implementing positive and constructive coping strategies.

Again, you don't have to try and use them all. Just try those that are relevant to you.

Let's start by looking at reducing your reliance on safety behaviours.

Reducing your reliance on safety behaviours

Safety behaviours are actions that we take to make us feel more comfortable with a situation that we are anxious about. If I was to list as many types of safety behaviours as I could think of here, the list would be almost endless. But here are some key examples:

- avoidance
- escaping/leaving situations
- reassurance-seeking
- using something as a comfort when in an anxiety-provoking situation.

Have a go at the following safety behaviours activity so you can learn more about them.

MATCH THE SAFETY BEHAVIOUR

Grant is 17 years old and gets anxious if he has to go into places where there are lots of people as he is worried that something bad will happen. See if you can match up Grant's use of safety behaviours with the categories of safety behaviours given.

SAFETY BEHAVIOUR CATEGORY	GRANT'S SAFETY BEHAVIOURS
AVOIDANCE	GRANT GETS HIS MUM TO GO INTO THE SUPERMARKET BEFORE HE DOES TO SEE HOW MANY PEOPLE ARE IN THERE. HE THEN ASKS HIS MUM LOTS OF QUESTIONS ABOUT WHETHER HE CAN COPE WITH THE NUMBER OF PEOPLE IN THE STORE.
REASSURANCE-SEEKING	BEFORE GRANT STARTS HIS SHOPPING, HE MENTALLY MAPS OUT THE QUICKEST ROUTE OUT OF THE SUPERMARKET.
OTHER COMFORT STRATEGIES	GRANT DOESN'T GO TO BIG SUPERMARKETS.
ESCAPE	GRANT HOLDS ONTO A TROLLEY EVEN IF HE ONLY NEEDS A FEW THINGS SO HE CAN FEEL LESS SHAKY. HE WILL ONLY GO INTO A SUPERMARKET IF HE HAS A BOTTLE OF WATER WITH HIM.

The answers to this activity can be found in the Appendix.

Safety behaviours are a short-term way of keeping our anxiety low. However, in the long term, they feed our Anxiety Gremlin.

For example, if we have a phobia about supermarkets and *avoid* visiting supermarkets, we don't have to experience the anxiety that visiting one might create. BUT, if Grant always *avoided* big supermarkets, he would never get to see that he could cope with being in one and that nothing bad happens.

Also, relying on certain *comfort* or *reassurance-seeking* safety behaviours can help in the initial stages of dealing with your anxiety as they can enable you to enter situations that you would normally avoid. BUT if Grant always relies on *comfort* behaviours like holding onto a trolley or on *reassurance-seeking* from his mum, he will believe that he can only cope with going into a supermarket because he used these safety behaviours. He won't get to see that he was strong enough to cope without them. He might also believe that nothing bad happened to him because of the safety behaviours and not because it was unlikely that anything bad would happen anyway.

And if Grant always *escapes* from a supermarket when his anxiety hits, he won't get to see that anxiety normally peaks and then calms down gradually if you make yourself stay in a situation. So it would be good for Grant to set himself targets to stay in the supermarket for longer periods of time each time he visits.

So to sum up, in the long run, safety behaviours keep the Anxiety Gremlin Cycle going as they feed our Anxiety Gremlins!

To help you get started with reducing your safety behaviours, fill in the Anxiety Box that follows listing:

- each safety behaviour you use
- their long-term negative effects
- whether they help you to feed or starve your Anxiety Gremlin
- what you can do to reduce the use of each safety behaviour.

ANXIETY BOX

MY SAFETY BEHAVIOURS	LONG-TERM NEGATIVE EFFECTS	DO THEY FEED OR STARVE MY GREMLIN?	HOW I CAN REDUCE THEM

Reducing compulsive behaviours

This section is particularly appropriate for someone who has OCD.

A compulsive behaviour is an action you feel you need to do in order to stop a bad thing from happening, such as checking doors are locked or putting your shoes in a certain order in your wardrobe. The problem with compulsive behaviours is that by doing them you:

- aren't allowing yourself to see that the behaviour and the bad thing you are worrying about aren't linked
- waste so much time and energy on them
- are feeding your Anxiety Gremlin.

Here's Cassie's story to help you see what I mean.

CASSIE'S SAYS CLEAR OFF TO HER COMPULSIONS!

Cassie is 13 years old. For as far back as she can remember she has been experiencing anxiety and compulsive behaviours. It started off with needing to put her toys in her room in a certain order, needing to have her clothes in a certain order in her wardrobe and wearing certain coloured socks on certain days. She was afraid that if she didn't do these things, bad things would happen.

As she got a bit older, every time she felt anxious she would pick something up that was around her, such as a leaf off the ground or a paperclip off the floor, and put it in her pocket. She would take that thing home and keep it in her room. Whenever her mum tried to throw these things out, Cassie would get extremely upset and anxious as she felt that keeping hold of these things was keeping her safe.

Now that she is 13 years old, the house is full of things that Cassie has hoarded and she won't let her family throw anything out. Cassie's compulsions now also include a belief that if she writes down or says certain numbers something bad will happen.

Eventually Cassie realised she needed help as the compulsions were taking over her life. Cassie needed a gradual plan to reduce her compulsions, as she couldn't just stop them overnight.

Cassie's plan

- Identify my compulsive behaviours.
- Wear a different colour of socks from what I believe it should be one day a week while reassuring myself that this is OK and that nothing bad will happen. Then gradually increase this step by step until I'm comfortable with wearing any colour of socks I want on any day.
- Change the order of one item of clothing in my wardrobe while reassuring myself that this is OK and that nothing bad will happen. Then gradually move more items around until eventually I can cope with my clothes being in a different order.
- Change the order of one toy in my room while reassuring myself that this is OK and that nothing bad will happen. Then gradually move more toys until I can cope with them being placed anywhere.
- Bin one item that I have hoarded each day while reassuring myself that this is OK and that nothing bad will happen.
- Challenge the link that I have made between certain numbers and bad things happening.
- Rate my anxiety each day on a scale of 1 to 10.
- Praise myself for achieving each target.

Cassie becomes a scientist!

Cassie found this process difficult, and it *is* difficult when you strongly believe that these compulsive acts will keep you and others safe from harm. But by reducing her compulsive behaviours bit by bit, Cassie became a scientist testing out the predictions that she had been making for years. In true scientific fashion, she managed to prove to herself that bad things don't happen just because you don't carry out one of these compulsive acts. She got to test out her predictions and develop new ones based on true evidence. Bit by bit, her anxiety reduced. Cassie is a fantastic example of someone who starved her Anxiety Gremlin bit by bit, step by step, until she was happier, healthier and living life without compulsions! She starved her Anxiety Gremlin. Well done Cassie!

And you can starve your Anxiety Gremlin too just like Cassie did! To help you do this, if you have any compulsions that you feel you have to act upon, list them in the Anxiety Box below and then list how you think you can start to reduce those compulsions.

ANXIETY BOX

MY COMPULSIONS	DO MY COMPULSIONS FEED OR STARVE MY GREMLIN?	HOW I CAN GRADUALLY REDUCE MY COMPULSIONS

Implementing positive and constructive coping strategies

Putting positive and constructive coping strategies into practice will help fill the void left by reducing your reliance on more negative coping strategies and on safety behaviours and compulsions. They will also help to starve your Anxiety Gremlin!

We're going to have a look at the following examples of positive coping strategies:

- behavioural experiments
- gradual exposure
- problem-solving
- worry time
- talking
- using relaxation and distraction techniques
- having fun and enjoyment
- being assertive
- living healthily
- using an anxiety diary.

BEHAVIOURAL EXPERIMENTS

As we saw when we discussed reducing compulsions, by testing out your fears and worst case scenario predictions, you will find out that your worst fears and predictions rarely ever happen. This will allow you to become more and more confident and starve your Anxiety Gremlin!

So you need to be like a scientist and design behavioural experiments to test out your predictions. For example, if you have anxiety about being sick in the cinema, try testing out that prediction by going into the cinema for a short period of time and gradually extend the length of time you stay in the cinema for.

Let's look at a scenario to see what behavioural experiment you would design for Leroy.

LEROY'S FEAR

Leroy is 14 years old. He worries about going into public places, especially those that are crowded. He is afraid that he will pick up germs from the people in the crowds and become really ill. He gets extremely anxious if he has to use a public toilet due to his fear of germs. He also fears that he might have a panic attack and stop breathing as he has had panic attacks in public places in the past. Leroy particularly worries about buses, trains, cinemas, shopping centres, supermarkets and concerts.

In the Anxiety Box below, design a behavioural experiment that Leroy could use to test out his anxious thoughts about public places.

ANXIETY BOX

Behavioural experiment for Leroy

One example of a behavioural experiment that you may have suggested is that Leroy spends short periods of time on a bus to see that he doesn't stop breathing.

Now think about a behavioural experiment you could use to test out an anxious prediction of your own. Write down your experiment idea in the Anxiety Box below.

ANXIETY BOX

My anxious prediction is:

I could use the following behavioural experiment to test out my anxious prediction:

GRADUAL EXPOSURE

Gradual exposure involves gradually facing your fears and worries by gradually putting yourself into situations that you would normally avoid because of your anxiety. The best way to do this is to develop what professionals call an *exposure ladder*.

Here's how to create an exposure ladder:

1. Write down the type of situation you get anxious about.
2. Draw a ladder.
3. On the bottom rung of the ladder, place the first thing you want to do to confront your anxiety. This needs to be the action that you will find the easiest to do.
4. On the top rung put the final step that you want to achieve.
5. Put other gradual steps on the rungs in between.
6. Start to perform each action on your ladder beginning with the action on the bottom rung.
7. As you tackle each action on your ladder, measure your anxiety (on a simple scale of 1 to 10).
8. Only move on to the next rung when you are ready to.
9. If you feel unable to do one of the actions, try breaking it down into smaller steps and tackle those bit by bit.
10. Reward and praise yourself for achieving each step.

Here's an example of an exposure ladder for Katrina, aged ten, who has a phobia of dogs.

EXPOSURE LADDER

ANXIOUS SITUATION – PHOBIA OF DOGS

Stroke a dog

Let a dog smell the back of my hand

Hold a dog's lead for a few seconds

Stand next to a dog without touching it

Move a bit closer again

Move a bit closer

Go out to the park and watch dogs from a distance

Watch a TV programme about dogs

In the next Anxiety Box, design your own exposure ladder if you feel this will help you to manage your anxiety and starve your Anxiety Gremlin.

ANXIETY BOX

MY EXPOSURE LADDER

PROBLEM-SOLVING

Difficult situations and problems do occur in life and it is normal to worry about them sometimes. However, getting anxious won't help you to resolve them. Problem-solving is a way of finding solutions to a problem in order to starve your Anxiety Gremlin.

When working out how to tackle a problem you need to:

- work out exactly what the problem is
- think about possible solutions to the problem
- look at the pros and cons of each solution approach
- decide which approach to take and implement it.

Let's see how you can apply the above strategies to a problem that someone else has in the following example.

WILL'S LIFE

Will is 15 years old. He is anxious as he has to hand in an assignment at school and he hasn't completed it on time because he has been visiting his mum in hospital every evening and helping his dad around the house. He is worried about his mum's ill health and his dad's ability to cope. His dad has been getting very irritable since his mum was diagnosed with her illness and has started to drink a bottle of wine most evenings.

Q. What problems is Will facing?

....

....

....

Q. What can Will do to help solve the problems that he is facing?

....

....

....

You may have suggested that Will talk to his teacher about his assignment and to his dad or someone else he can trust about his dad's behaviour.

WORRY TIME

'Worry time' is a specific time in the day that you can set aside to think about your worries. But this isn't about spending your time worrying for the sake of it. It's about:

- Identifying what is worrying you.
- Identifying what you can do to address your worries.
- Perhaps talking to someone else about your worries during this time or writing down your worries and what you are going to do about them.
- Setting a time limit for this process as the less time you spend on your worries, the less you feed your Anxiety Gremlin and then eventually the less worry time you will need.

If you think worry time could be useful for you, in the Anxiety Box given, write down when your worry time will be and set yourself some rules for your worry time. Remember to stick to these rules so you can help starve your Anxiety Gremlin!

ANXIETY BOX

Worry time and rules

TALKING

Talking is an important anxiety management tool as it can help you to:

EXPRESS HOW YOU ARE FEELING	CHALLENGE YOUR THOUGHTS	IDENTIFY WAYS TO RESOLVE PROBLEMS

Q. Which of the following people do you think you could talk to when you are anxious?

MUM	DAD	FRIEND
BROTHER/SISTER	OTHER RELATIVE	TEACHER

Q. Are there any other people that you would talk to that aren't mentioned in the previous question? If so, write them down below.

....

....

....

Don't forget you can talk to a professional, such as a doctor, psychologist or counsellor about things that are concerning you either face to face or through a telephone helpline. There are also many support groups available where you can talk to people who are in similar circumstances to you. Your doctor, school or college may be able to put you in touch with these forms of support. Remember talking can help you to starve your Anxiety Gremlin.

USING RELAXATION AND DISTRACTION TECHNIQUES

You can use simple relaxation techniques, such as deep breathing exercises, to help you to relax when you're feeling anxious. These can be helpful when you are trying to face your worries during the gradual exposure and behavioural experiments that we discussed earlier in this chapter. They are also excellent ways of starving your Anxiety Gremlin.

Have a go at the following exercises. It's OK if these don't feel right to you as they aren't always suitable for everybody. But give them a go and see what you think. Remember you can always try other forms of activity that are aimed at relaxation such as:

- Meditation and yoga: the word 'yoga' originates from the Sanskrit word 'Yuj', meaning to join or unite. Yoga aims to create balance and harmony in your body and mind through breathing, yoga exercise poses and meditation. Meditation involves focusing on quiet thoughts and contemplations to help you free your mind of distractions and stresses. There are different forms of both yoga and meditation.
- T'ai Chi: originating in the martial arts, T'ai Chi is now practised as a form of exercise that combines deep breathing with slow and gentle movements in order to achieve a relaxed state of mind and body.

DEEP BREATHING EXERCISE

Either sit down or lie down on your back. Focus on your breathing. Put one hand on your upper chest and one on your abdomen (just below your ribs). Gently breathe in, and as you do so, notice that your abdomen rises slowly under your hand. Slowly breathe out noticing how your abdomen falls down slowly. Repeat the process, breathing in and out with a slow, steady rhythm. You are breathing correctly if your hand on your abdomen moves up and down slowly but the hand on your chest remains still.

RELAXATION EXERCISE 1

Close your eyes and imagine yourself somewhere peaceful, happy or enjoyable. Somewhere that makes you feel relaxed and happy. Focus on that image, start to build the detail, and for a short time, imagine that you are actually there. Breathe deeply and slowly as you do.

RELAXATION EXERCISE 2

Focus on one muscle in your body at a time, and slowly tighten and then relax the muscle.

RELAXATION EXERCISE 3

Lie on your back. Breathe in deeply and slowly, imagining that the breath is coming in through the soles of your feet, travelling up through your body and exiting through your head. Breathe in again and this time imagine that the breath is coming in through your head, travelling down through your body and out through the soles of your feet. Repeat this exercise several times slowly.

VISUALISATION EXERCISES

- Imagine a calming image.
- Imagine a funny image.
- Imagine you are in a happy place.
- Imagine your worries as visual things being discarded by you.
- Imagine yourself tackling a worrying situation and what it would look like and feel like.

Alternatively, you can use activities that you enjoy to help you relax. These same activities can also be good to help you:

- take your mind off anxious thoughts that might be whirring around in your head
- stop focusing on your physical symptoms when you are having a panic attack
- stop you checking your body for negative physical symptoms when you experience health anxiety
- take your mind off the urge to act upon a compulsion.

And they also help you to starve your Anxiety Gremlin!

But in order for them to work as a distraction, the activities that you choose need to be able to fully absorb your attention. Have a go at coming up with relaxation and distraction activities that might work for you and write them down in the Anxiety Box below.

ANXIETY BOX

Positive things I can do to relax when I'm anxious

Positive things I can do to distract myself when I'm anxious

Examples that you might have included in your list are:

- breathing and relaxation techniques
- exercise
- T'ai Chi
- yoga and meditation
- hot bath/shower
- listening to music
- watching TV
- spending time with friends or family
- volunteering
- extra-curricular/leisure activities
- going to the cinema
- reading.

HAVING FUN AND ENJOYMENT

It is also important to ensure that you:

- get time for you every day
- give yourself things to look forward to
- increase your positive activity levels
- try new positive challenges
- have fun!

All of these will help you to realise that life doesn't have to be all about anxiety and worry! They will also give you the opportunity to feel more positive about yourself and your life and to starve your Anxiety Gremlin.

Q. Name one positive and enjoyable new activity you could add to your life and routine at the moment.

....

BEING ASSERTIVE

As human beings, we all have certain rights.

Q. List three rights you think you have as a human.

....

....

....

You may have written three of the following or you may have picked other rights which are just as valid:

- to be treated with respect
- to say 'No!'
- to have choice
- to be listened to
- to not be physically harmed by others
- to express your opinions
- to ask for help.

When you are assertive, you recognise that your rights are equal to those of other people and you respect your own rights and the rights of others. Thus, being assertive involves:

SELF-BELIEF	RESPECTING THE RIGHTS, FEELINGS, OPINIONS AND NEEDS OF OTHERS
EXPRESSING YOUR OWN THOUGHTS, FEELINGS, OPINIONS AND NEEDS IN A CALM AND RESPECTFUL WAY	STANDING UP FOR YOUR RIGHTS IN A CALM AND RESPECTFUL WAY

These assertiveness skills are helpful to anxiety management in a number of ways, including helping you to:

- say ‘No!’ in response to unrealistic pressures or demands that are triggering anxiety
- solve problems
- reach resolutions or compromises
- ask for help
- make complaints
- deal with conflict
- and starve your Anxiety Gremlin!

LIVING HEALTHILY

Our lifestyles can also impact upon our anxiety levels so living healthily can help us to starve our Anxiety Gremlin. It is important to:

- EAT A HEALTHY BALANCED DIET AND HAVE REGULAR MEALS
- REDUCE THE AMOUNT OF STIMULANTS IN YOUR DIET, INCLUDING CAFFEINE AND SUGAR
- DO REGULAR EXERCISE BUT NOT TOO MUCH
- GET ADEQUATE SLEEP

All of the above are natural ways to help us feel a bit calmer. For example, exercise helps to use up some of the adrenalin that is released when we get anxious.

Sleep hygiene techniques can help you to improve your sleep when you are experiencing sleep problems as a symptom of your anxiety. These include:

SLEEP ENVIRONMENT – look at what changes you may need to make to your sleep environment, such as noise levels, light levels, colours in the room, type of bed/mattress, heat levels, distractions in the room (e.g. mobile phone or TV).

PRE-BED ROUTINE – avoid anything too stimulating before bed. Do things that help you to relax instead.

SLEEP ROUTINE – getting up at approximately the same time and going to bed at approximately the same time each day can help you to sleep better.

EATING – eat at regular times as our body clock is also influenced by eating times. Also avoid stimulants as they can disturb sleep patterns.

EXERCISE – ensure you have done some physical activity in the day, but don't do aerobic exercise too close to bedtime as it stimulates the system.

IF YOU CAN'T SLEEP – get out of bed and do something relaxing and when you feel tired go back to bed and try to sleep again. Don't worry about not being able to sleep as this will only make things worse.

If you are having problems with your sleep, write down what changes you think you need to make to improve your sleep in the next Anxiety Box. Remember these will also help you to starve your Anxiety Gremlin!

ANXIETY BOX

Strategies to help improve my sleep

USING AN ANXIETY DIARY

There is one final tool to look at that might help you when you're trying to put all the strategies into practice, namely an *Anxiety Diary*. It can also help you to starve your Anxiety Gremlin. Let's take a look at an example.

MY ANXIETY DIARY

Date ....

The trigger ....

What was I thinking?

....
....

How was I feeling physically?

....
....

How was I feeling emotionally?

....
....

How did I act?

....
....

What were the consequences?

....
....

Did I feed or starve my Anxiety Gremlin?

Feed Starve

If I fed my Anxiety Gremlin, what could I have done differently?

....

....

If I starved my Anxiety Gremlin, how did I do this and what does my success at managing my anxiety tell me about me?

....

....

....

....

....

....

10

Anxiety Dos and Don'ts

Now it's time for you to think about everything we have gone through so far. Think about all the negative ways and all the positive and constructive ways of reacting to anxiety triggers that you have learnt about. From these, I want you to come up with your own personal list of Anxiety Dos and Don'ts and write them in the box that follows. Try and come up with at least five of each! Then write down the effects that you think these Dos and Don'ts would have on you and the people around you.

Some people find it helpful to carry this list around with them in their bag or to put a copy of it up on their wall at home so that they can look at it and remind themselves of what to do at times when they are finding their anxiety difficult to manage. Remember... the things that you put in your Dos column need to be things that will starve your Anxiety Gremlin.

ANXIETY BOX

DOS	DON'TS
EFFECTS	**EFFECTS**

Here's an example of a Dos and Don'ts list from Rafiq aged 14.

Dos

Keep calm

Do things to relax

Distractions

Think realistically

Think positively about me

Remember that the bad thing I'm worrying about is unlikely to happen

Challenge any thoughts that aren't based on facts

Tackle problems

Talk to my friends about my problems

Go out more

Realise that I can cope with life

Realise that not everything will go wrong

Effects

Starve my Anxiety Gremlin

Be less anxious

Be calm

Be happy

Be more confident

Have more fun in life

Be more likely to achieve what I want to

Be healthier physically and mentally

Worry my family less

Don'ts

Avoid! Avoid! Avoid!

Thinking things are worse than they are

Thinking about what if this and what if that

Disaster movie thinking

Thinking I'm stupid and useless

Thinking I can't cope

Thinking that bad things will happen

Drinking to cope

Self-harming

Hide in my room

Effects

Feed my Anxiety Gremlin

Anxiety, anxiety, anxiety!

Low self-confidence

Unhappy

Upset

Overwhelmed

Can't cope

Harming myself physically

Cause my family worry and stress

Never see my friends

Feel like I can't leave the house

Beat myself up

Blame myself for everything

Feel ashamed and guilty

Now you have learnt a range of anxiety management techniques and have come up with your own list of anxiety Dos and Don'ts, try the following activity. In the next Anxiety Box, write down your anxiety triggers list again and then write down what you can do in response to each trigger.

ANXIETY BOX

MY TRIGGERS	HOW I CAN RESPOND TO MY TRIGGERS

11

Summing Up

We have now gone through all the methods you may need to starve your Anxiety Gremlin and get your anxiety under control. It's now down to you to put them into practice. But don't forget you may not need them all. Just work on implementing those that are relevant to you and your anxiety.

REMEMBER...

Only YOU can change how you react!

YOU'RE the one in control of your anxious reactions!

YOU have all the power to starve your Anxiety Gremlin!

Let's have a quick recap before we finish.

Write down five things that you have learnt about your anxiety and how to control it in the Anxiety Box below.

ANXIETY BOX

What I have learnt

Now try applying your new knowledge to the last time you were anxious. Answer the questions in the Anxiety Box below and be proud of just how much you have learnt about your anxiety and how to starve your Anxiety Gremlin!

ANXIETY BOX

Think about a recent time when you were anxious, that you wish you had handled better.

Q. What happened?

....

....

Q. How did you think about the situation?

....

....

Q. How did you feel?

....

....

Q. How did you act?

....

....

Q. What effects did it have on you and other people?

....

....

Q. How could you have handled it differently?

....

....

Let's also check what you have learnt by taking an Anxiety Quiz!

THE ANXIETY QUIZ!

1. Fight, Flight .... Response. What is the missing word?

a) Melt ☐

b) Freeze ☐

c) Refrigerate ☐

2. Name three physical signs of anxiety.

1. ....

2. ....

3. ....

3. Which of the following can affect your ability to control your anxiety or make you more susceptible to developing anxiety?

a) Past experiences ☐

b) Your beliefs about yourself and the world ☐

c) Learning from other people ☐

d) Drug use ☐

e) Other mental health issues ☐

f) All of the above ☐

4. Name three types of anxiety thinking errors.

1. ....

2. ....

3. ....

5. Name three unconstructive ways to act when you get anxious.

1. ....

2. ....

3. ....

6. Name the five parts of the Anxiety Gremlin Cycle.

1. ....

2. ....

3. ....

4. ....

5. ....

7. Name two aspects of your life that your anxiety can affect.

1. ....

2. ....

8. What do you need to do to your Anxiety Gremlin?

a) Feed it ☐

b) Starve it ☐

9. Name three ways to starve your Anxiety Gremlin.

1. ....

2. ....

3. ....

10. Unravel this word to make a type of anxiety disorder.

HBIOPA ....

11. Write down one question you should ask yourself when you begin to get anxious.

....

12. Fill in the missing word.

Disaster .... thinking

13. Who is in control of your anxiety?

a) A place ☐

b) Another person ☐

c) An event ☐

d) You ☐

Turn to the Appendix to see how you got on!

Well done! I'm sure you did great!

Now have a go at a more creative way of reinforcing what you have learnt with the following activity.

YOUR VOICE! TEACHING OTHER YOUNG PEOPLE ABOUT ANXIETY

If you wanted to spread the word far and wide to other young people about anxiety and how to manage it, what would you do?

Pick whether you would:

- design a webpage for young people to access
- design a poster campaign for schools and colleges
- design scenes for a TV advert
- give a talk at schools and colleges
- deliver a play at school and colleges.

Then, in the space below, jot down ideas on the kinds of things you would include in whichever type of campaign method you would use. And if you want to have a go at completing your campaign advert, website, poster, etc., on some separate paper or on a computer go ahead. Just think, maybe your school or college might want to use it!

Now let's check on how your anxiety has changed during the course of reading this book by re-taking the My Anxiety Questionnaire. Plus there are now two extra questions at the end!

MY ANXIETY QUESTIONNAIRE

1. How often do you feel anxious? Tick which answer applies to you.

a) Most of the time ☐

b) Often ☐

c) Sometimes ☐

d) Rarely ☐

e) Never ☐

2. How long have you been experiencing anxiety for? Tick which answer applies to you.

a) For as long as I can remember ☐

b) For years ☐

c) For months ☐

d) For weeks ☐

3. Think about how you tend to feel physically when you get anxious. Highlight or colour in any of the following that apply to you.

- TINGLING OR NUMB LIPS
- HEADACHES
- HAIR LOSS
- DIZZINESS
- RED FACE
- CHOKING SENSATION
- DRY MOUTH
- LUMP IN THROAT
- RINGING IN EARS
- GRINDING TEETH
- HEART RACING OR PALPITATIONS
- RAPID OR SHALLOW BREATHING
- CHEST TIGHTNESS OR PAIN
- SHORTNESS OF BREATH OR CAN'T CATCH BREATH
- STOMACH ACHE OR BUTTERFLIES
- NAUSEA
- SKIN PROBLEMS
- WEIGHT LOSS OR GAIN
- BOWEL PROBLEMS
- LACK OF APPETITE
- FREQUENT URINATION
- SHAKING OR TREMORS
- HOT
- TIREDNESS
- COLD
- SLEEP DISTURBANCE
- JELLY LEGS
- FAINTING
- SWEATING
- TWITCHES OR TICS
- MUSCLE PAIN, ACHE OR TENSION
- NUMBNESS OR TINGLING IN LIMBS

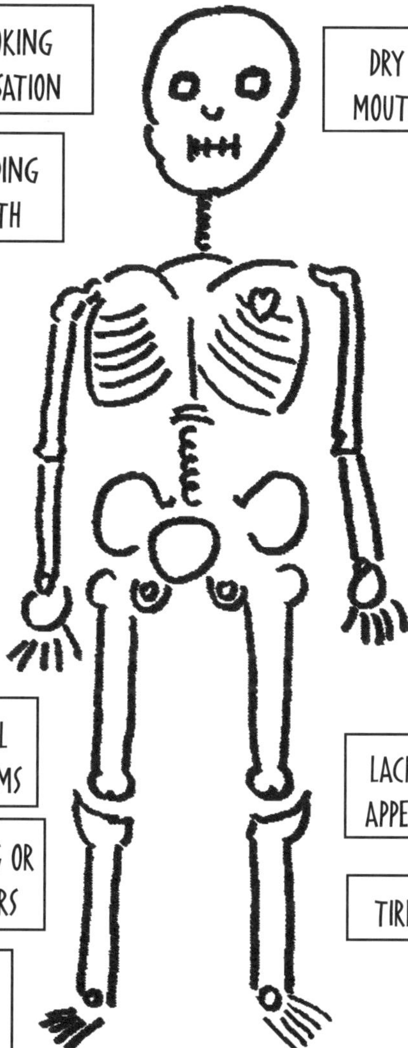

4. **Rate the following possible sources of anxiety on a scale of 0 to 10.**

   0 = You experience no anxiety in response to that source.

   10 = You experience a high level of anxiety in response to that source.

POTENTIAL SOURCE	RATING	POTENTIAL SOURCE	RATING
School/college		Work	
Family		Friendships	
Leaving the house		Enclosed spaces	
Untidiness		Germs/ contamination	
Boyfriend/girlfriend		Others' expectations of you	
Performing/ speaking in groups		Travelling by car/bus/train/ plane/boat	
Bullying		Change	
Animals/ insects/birds		The dark	
Expectations of self		Peer pressure	
Social situations		Crowded places	
The future		Your health	
How you look		Being perfect	

POTENTIAL SOURCE	RATING	POTENTIAL SOURCE	RATING
Health of others		Actions of others	
Problems at home		Living environment	
Crime and safety		Attitudes of others	
Parties		Public places	
Storms		Injections/needles	
Being away from family		Harm to others	
What other people think of you		How well you achieve at things in life	
Your responsibilities		The media	
Things being unlucky		Fire	
Getting into trouble		Worrying about worrying	
Using the telephone		Being alone	
Heights		Food	
World news		Exams	
Blood		Things going wrong	
Death		Visiting doctor or dentist	
Water		Speaking to people	

5. Do you ever act in any of the following ways when you get anxious? Tick any that apply.

- ☐ Avoid things
- ☐ Self-harm
- ☐ Do things to get people's attention
- ☐ Seek reassurance from others
- ☐ Avoid leaving the house
- ☐ Put off doing things
- ☐ Hide away from people, such as friends or family
- ☐ Deny you have a problem
- ☐ Check for signs of danger
- ☐ Binge eat
- ☐ Drink excessively
- ☐ Get other people to do things for you
- ☐ Skip meals
- ☐ Plan escape routes out of places or situations
- ☐ Act irritably towards people
- ☐ Make mistakes
- ☐ Only go out if accompanied
- ☐ Skip school/college
- ☐ Cry
- ☐ Act aggressively
- ☐ Check yourself for physical signs of anxiety or illness
- ☐ Stay in bed
- ☐ Ignore problems
- ☐ Take drugs
- ☐ Get annoyed with self
- ☐ Make yourself sick after eating
- ☐ Leave situations
- ☐ Follow rituals or routines obsessively

6. Are there any other ways that you tend to act when anxious that aren't on the previous list? If so, write them down here.

....

....

....

....

7. Do any of the following thought patterns apply to you when you are anxious? Highlight or colour in any that apply.

- 'WHAT IF?' THOUGHTS
- NEGATIVE THOUGHTS ABOUT YOURSELF
- THOUGHTS ABOUT WORST CASE SCENARIOS
- 'I CAN'T' THOUGHTS
- UNREALISTIC EXPECTATIONS OF YOURSELF
- THOUGHTS ABOUT HARMING YOURSELF
- THOUGHTS WHERE YOU JUMP TO CONCLUSIONS
- THINKING THAT THINGS ARE WORSE THAN THEY ACTUALLY ARE
- UNREALISTIC THOUGHTS ABOUT SITUATIONS
- THINKING THAT THINGS WILL BE WORSE THAN THEY ARE LIKELY TO BE
- FOCUSING ON NEGATIVES ABOUT SITUATIONS
- OBSESSIVE THOUGHTS
- THOUGHTS THAT EXAGGERATE BADNESS
- THOUGHTS WHERE YOU BLOW THINGS OUT OF PROPORTION
- THOUGHTS THAT EXAGGERATE DANGER
- SELF-BLAMING THOUGHTS
- THOUGHTS THAT EXAGGERATE LIKELIHOOD OF THINGS HAPPENING
- THOUGHTS WHERE YOU COMPARE YOURSELF NEGATIVELY TO OTHERS
- PREDICTING WHAT OTHER PEOPLE ARE THINKING
- SELF-DOUBTING THOUGHTS
- OVER-GENERALISING THOUGHTS

8. How often do you experience panic attacks when anxious? Tick which answer applies to you.

a) Often ☐ c) Rarely ☐

b) Sometimes ☐ d) Never ☐

9. Do you ever find it harder to remember things or concentrate on things when you are anxious? Circle your answer.

a) Yes b) No

10. Which of the following words do you associate with your anxiety? Highlight or colour in any that apply to you.

WORRIED	ON EDGE	PANICKY
NERVOUS	AFRAID	TRAPPED
FULL OF DREAD	RESTLESS	TENSE

11. **Do you ever feel any of the following as a result of your anxiety? Highlight or colour in any that apply to you.**

UPSET

WORTHLESS

AGITATED

SUSPICIOUS OF OTHERS

UNDER PRESSURE

LONELY

GUILTY

ASHAMED

LOW IN CONFIDENCE

OVERWHELMED

IRRITABLE

LOW IN MOOD

ANGRY

CONFUSED

OUT OF CONTROL

DEFENSIVE

INSECURE

STRESSED

LIKE A FAILURE

UNHAPPY

EMBARRASSED

12. **Does your anxiety have any negative effects on any of the following aspects of your life? Highlight or colour in any that apply.**

Physical health	Mental health and emotional wellbeing
Family relationships	Friendships
Performance at school/college/work/leisure activities	
Motivation to do things	Romantic relationships

13. Do you believe your anxiety is in or out of your control? Circle your answer.

a) In my control b) Out of my control

14. Have you seen any changes in your anxiety since you completed the My Anxiety Questionnaire at the start of the book? Circle your answer.

a) Yes b) No

15. If you have seen changes in your anxiety, what are these changes?

....

....

I hope that you have seen your anxiety levels start to reduce and the way you are responding to potential anxiety triggers starting to change too. As you continue to put everything you have learnt from this book into practice, occasionally ask yourself the questions from the My Anxiety Questionnaire to monitor how far you've progressed and how well you're starving your Anxiety Gremlin!

Please be patient with yourself when putting all you've learnt into practice. You won't change everything overnight and remember no one gets it right all the time. No one is perfect!

Also keep re-visiting the activities in this book to help you along the way. And here are two final activities before we finish.

Your anxiety management goals

Q. What goals would you like to set yourself so that you can continue to improve your ability to manage your anxiety?

....

....

....

....

Anxiety agony aunt or uncle

Sarah is 15 years old. She can't stop wondering what other people are thinking of her all the time. She worries when she has to go to family events, like weddings and christenings, because she believes she will do something to make a fool of herself. She worries when she has to go to parties or to the cinema with her friends in case she does something that will make them think she is stupid. She worries when she has to stand up and talk in front of people at school in case she makes a mistake. It takes her ages to leave the house to go to school or to go out with her friends because she worries so much about how she looks. She also worries that her friends don't really like her and about whether they are saying nasty things about her behind her back. She can't get these thoughts out of her mind when she lies in bed at night, so she doesn't sleep very well.

What advice would you give to Sarah? Write your advice in the box below.

ANXIETY BOX

Dear Sarah...

Just a few final words from me:

Sometimes life can be difficult. But you are in control of how you react when anxiety triggers come along.

You are in control of your anxiety and you can starve your Anxiety Gremlin!

Just believe in you!

Good luck!

Appendix: Quiz Answers

ANXIETY WORD SEARCH

D	R	E	A	D	X	W	Q	R	Z	S
D	C	J	K	T	W	X	V	S	S	P
W	U	B	G	E	A	Z	A	E	M	J
O	V	H	J	N	P	M	N	W	X	O
V	T	G	U	S	J	S	K	Z	Q	B
W	Z	C	K	I	U	I	M	L	Z	A
O	X	U	S	O	M	Q	F	O	P	L
R	O	A	V	N	L	G	E	Q	D	S
R	E	R	A	Q	M	B	A	H	J	E
Y	E	C	T	Y	P	C	R	F	R	U
N	F	R	Y	P	M	P	A	N	I	C

ANXIETY DISORDERS CROSSWORD

ACROSS

1. Agoraphobia
8. Separation
9. Health
10. See 4 down
12. See 4 down

DOWN

2. Generalised
3. See 7 down
4. Obsessive (4 down) compulsive (12 across) disorder (10 across)
5. Anxiety
6. Specific
7. Panic (7 down) attack (3 down)
11. Social

MATCH THE SCENARIOS

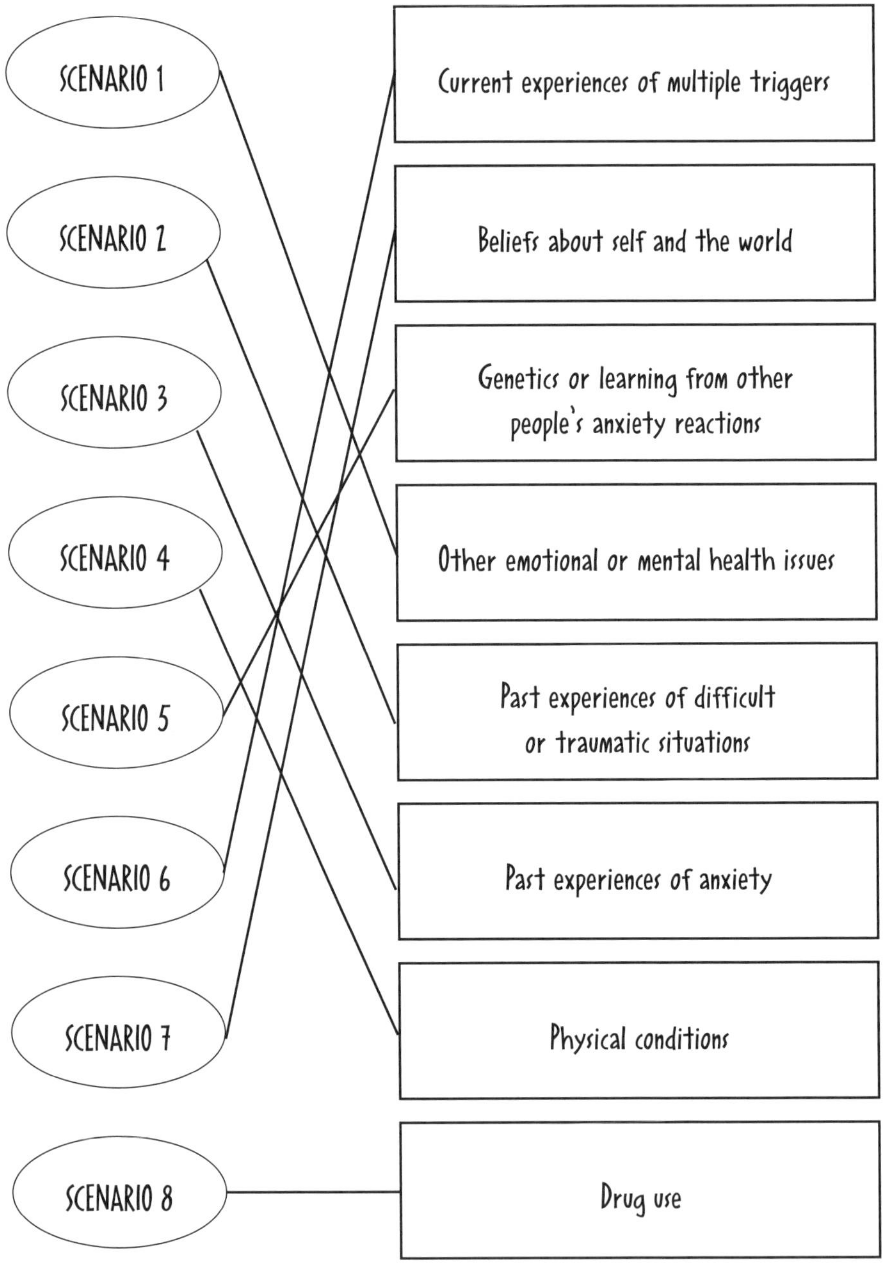

MATCH THE SAFETY BEHAVIOUR

SAFETY BEHAVIOUR CATEGORY

AVOIDANCE

REASSURANCE-SEEKING

OTHER COMFORT STRATEGIES

ESCAPE

GRANT'S SAFETY BEHAVIOURS

GRANT GETS HIS MUM TO GO INTO THE SUPERMARKET BEFORE HE DOES TO SEE HOW MANY PEOPLE ARE IN THERE. HE THEN ASKS HIS MUM LOTS OF QUESTIONS ABOUT WHETHER HE CAN COPE WITH THE NUMBER OF PEOPLE IN THE STORE.

BEFORE GRANT STARTS HIS SHOPPING, HE MENTALLY MAPS OUT THE QUICKEST ROUTE OUT OF THE SUPERMARKET.

GRANT DOESN'T GO TO BIG SUPERMARKETS.

GRANT HOLDS ONTO A TROLLEY EVEN IF HE ONLY NEEDS A FEW THINGS SO HE CAN FEEL LESS SHAKY. HE WILL ONLY GO INTO A SUPERMARKET IF HE HAS A BOTTLE OF WATER WITH HIM.

THE ANXIETY QUIZ

1. (b) Freeze.
2. You may have included any physical symptoms from the list on page 23, such as sweating, headaches and heart racing.
3. (f) All of the above.
4. You may have included any thought errors from the box on page 88, such as blowing things out of proportion, blaming yourself and 'what if?' thinking.
5. You may have included some of the behaviours from the list on page 24, such as avoidance, planning escape routes and skipping meals.
6. Trigger, thoughts, physical symptoms, emotions and behaviours.
7. You may have included any of the effects from those given on page 73, such as physical health and relationships.
8. (b) Starve it!
9. You may have included any of the eight steps towards managing your anxiety given on pages 78–79, such as understanding how anxiety occurs. You may have also included any of the managing thoughts and managing behaviours discussed in Chapters 9 and 10, such as thinking realistically and reducing compulsive behaviours.
10. Phobia
11. You may have included any of the questions in the thought bubbles on pages 89–90, such as 'Are my thoughts based on thinking errors?'
12. Movie.
13. (d) You.

REFERENCES

Barrett, P., Healy-Farrell, L. and March, J.S. (2004) 'Cognitive-behavioural family treatment of childhood obsessive compulsive disorder: a controlled trial.' *Journal of the American Academy of Child and Adolescent Psychiatry 43*, 1, 46–62.

Beck, A. T. (1976) *Cognitive Therapy and Emotional Disorders*. New York: International Universities Press.

Cartwright-Hatton, S., Roberts, C., Chitsabesan, P., *et al.* (2004) 'Systematic review of the efficacy of cognitive behaviour therapies for childhood and adolescent anxiety disorders.' *British Journal of Clinical Psychology 43*, 421–36.

Ellis, A. (1962) *Reason and Emotion in Psychotherapy*. New York: Lyle-Stuart.

Green, H., McGinnity, A., Meltzer, H., Ford, T. and Goodman, R. (2005) *Mental Health of Children and Young People in Great Britain 2004*. London: Office for National Statistics Publication, Palgrave MacMillan.

James, A.A.C.J., Soler, A. and Weatherall, R.R.W. (2005) 'Cognitive behavioural therapy for anxiety disorders in children and adolescents.' *Cochrane Database of Systematic Reviews 2005*, Issue 4. Art. No.: CD004690. DOI: 10.1002/14651858.CD004690.pub2. Published online January 2009.

Kazdin, A.E. and Weisz, J.R. (1998) 'Identifying and developing empirically supported child and adolescent treatments.' *Journal of Consulting and Clinical Psychology 66*, 19–36.

Kendall, P.C., Flannery-Schroeder, E., Panichelli-Mindel, S.M., Sotham-Gerow, M., Henin, A. and Warman, M. (1997) 'Therapy with youths with anxiety disorders: a second randomized clinical trial.' *Journal of Consulting and Clinical Psychology 18*, 255–70.

Kendall, P.C., Safford, S., Flannery-Schroeder, E. and Webb, A. (2004) 'Child anxiety treatment: Outcomes in adolescence and impact on substance abuse and depression at 7.4 year follow-up.' *Journal of Consulting and Clinical Psychology 72*, 276–287.

King, N.J., Molloy, G.N., Heyme, D., Murphy, G.C. and Ollendick, T. (1998) 'Emotive imagery treatment for childhood phobias: a credible and empirically validated intervention?' *Behavioural and Cognitive Psychotherapy 26*, 103–13.

Klein, J.B., Jacobs, R.H. and Reinecke, M.A. (2007) 'A meta-analysis of CBT in adolescents with depression.' *Journal of the American Academy of Child and Adolescent Psychiatry 46*, 1403–1413.

Lewinsohn, P.M. and Clarke, G.N. (1999) 'Psychosocial treatments for adolescent depression.' *Clinical Psychology Review 19*, 329–42.

National Institute for Clinical Excellence (NICE) (2005) 'Depression in Children and Young People. Identification and Management in Primary, Community and Secondary Care.' *Clinical Guideline 28*. Available at www.nice.org.uk/guidance/CG28, accessed on 2 January 2013.

National Institute for Clinical Excellence (NICE) (2005) 'Obsessive Compulsive Disorder: core interventions in the treatment of obsessive compulsive disorder and body dysmorphic disorder.' *Clinical Guideline 31*. Available at www.nice.org.uk/nicemedia/pdf/CG031niceguideline.pdf, accessed on 2 January 2012.

NSPCC (2004) *Someone to Turn To? Who Can Children and Young People Trust When They are Worried and Need to Talk?* London: NSPCC.

O'Kearney, R.T., Anstey, K., von Sanden, C. and Hunt, A. (2006) 'Behavioural and cognitive behavioural therapy for obsessive compulsive disorder in children and adolescents.' *Cochrane Database of Systematic Reviews 2006*, Issue 4. Art. No.: CD004856. DOI: 10.1002/14651858.CD004856.pub2. Published online January 2010.

Pavlov, I. P. (1927) *Conditioned Reflexes: An Investigation of the Physiological Activity of the Cerebral Cortex*. Translated and edited by G. V. Anrep. London: Oxford University Press.

Rapee, R.M., Wignall, A., Hudson, J.L. and Schniering, C.A. (2000) *Treating Anxious Children and Adolescents: An Evidence-Based Approach*. Oakland, CA: New Harbinger Publications.

Silverman, W.K., Kurtines, W.M., Ginsburg, G.S., Weems, C.F., Rabian, B. and Setafini, L.T. (1999) 'Contingency management, self-control and education support in the treatment of childhood phobic disorders: a randomized clinical trial.' *Journal of Consulting and Clinical Psychology 67*, 675–87.

Singleton, N., Bumpstead, R., O'Brien, M., Lee, A. and Meltzer, H. (2001) 'Psychiatric morbidity among adults living in private households' *National Statistics 154*. London: The Stationery Office.

Skinner, B. F. (1938) *The Behavior of Organisms*. New York: Appleton-Century-Crofts.

Spence, S., Donovan, C. and Brechman-Toussaint, M. (2000) 'The treatment of childhood social phobia: the effectiveness of a social skills training-based cognitive behavioural intervention with and without parental involvement.' *Journal of Child Psychology and Psychiatry 41*, 713–26.

This is to certify that

....

has successfully completed the
Starving the Anxiety Gremlin
workbook and can expertly

STARVE THEIR ANXIETY GREMLIN!